MUSINGS

of a

98 YEAR OLD SCIENTIST

John E. Burgener

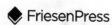

FriesenPress

Suite 300 - 990 Fort St
Victoria, BC, V8V 3K2
Canada

www.friesenpress.com

Copyright © 2020 by John A. Burgener
First Edition — 2020

ISBN
978-1-4602-9291-4 (Hardcover)
978-1-4602-9292-1 (Paperback)
978-1-4602-9293-8 (eBook)

Biography & Autobiography, Science & Technology

Distributed to the trade by The Ingram Book Company

Table of Contents

Foreword

With more time to ponder, I have spent some time remembering and thinking about the world today and tomorrow. At 98 years, I have seen a lot, done a lot, and thought a lot. Some musings on my childhood are included for the younger people, who may be interested in what was going on almost a hundred years ago. And, of course, I think it is important to reflect on how the past led to the present. Other musings are for those who might also be interested in the thoughts of a thinker who has had almost one hundred years to think. Of course, I have opinions on what is happening today, but my opinions may be somewhat different than most currently think as my past is different than that of most people alive today.

This work is a collection of some of my thoughts. It is the musings of a 98-year-old physicist, entrepreneur, traveller, husband, father, grandfather, and great-grandfather. I hope the reader will find things of interest, enlightening, and of value.

John E. Burgener

NOTE FROM THE EDITOR

My father, John Ernest Burgener, died on May 13, 2016, at the age of 99 years and a few months. The last main activity he worked on was this book—a product of several years of effort. He sent in his draft to FriesenPress on April 25, 2016. He had less than two weeks of painting, watching some movies, some listening to André Rieu's music, and some discussions with me on adding some more sections to this book—which he decided he did not want to do. He went to the hospital with a bladder infection, and while there had a heart attack that left him very weak. He did not recover and died from it a few days later.

We spent most of my life enjoying many heated debates on various topics. When I was a child, we almost always had dinner together as a family and the conversations covered all topics one can imagine. Dad and Mom discussed topics with us as though we were adults, from as far back as I can remember. His knowledge was vast, and he continued studying topics using the Internet as a wonderful resource in his last years. At 99, his mind remained sharp, and our discussions were often challenging for me as I often disagreed with him. To the best of my ability, I have finished editing this book with his views intact. While some of his views seem to me to be a reflection of his upbringing rather than of his logic, yet, my views on topics often relate to his teaching me to be open-minded on all topics and to trust logic more than tradition. I leave it to the reader to consider his views and thoughts and to ponder what are generally well-thought-out opinions and observations, but to remain considerate that his views were established almost 100 years ago and some biases remain from that time.

In his musing on how he got to live such a long life, he wrote: "I really think it is up to God. God wanted me to write some books and will keep me alive until I have done what he wants." I find it perfectly fitting that it was three weeks after he submitted the draft to be published that God decided that his work was finished, and it was time for him to head off to Heaven. I think you will notice that the book reflects well his understanding that God was part of everything he did, and that his life was about serving God and everyone else as best he could.

When Mom became senile, Dad insisted on being her primary caregiver, not letting her go to a nursing home. Ontario's medical system was destroying her, so, in 2008, he moved them to Nelson, BC, to live with my brother Paul for a year, then to Calgary to live with my brother Peter. But they longed to be home—so in 2010, at the age of 93, they moved back to Mississauga. They stayed in a retirement residence until Mom died, and then Dad wanted back into his old apartment in south Mississauga—he did not enjoy living with a bunch of old folks. So he moved again, in 2013, to an apartment on his own, with a roommate who helped when necessary but generally let Dad live on his own.

In the last few years, he struggled to write his musings. His eyes were failing, and he had to use a magnifying glass to see what was on the screen of his computer even though he used very large fonts, so he was often looking at one letter at a time. He had diabetes, which was slowly reducing the circulation in his arms and legs, and had trouble using his fingers, or getting up and walking. His mind remained sharp to the end—but his body was slowly decomposing. It was not a surprise when he had his heart attack, but his death leaves a void in the world. I hope that this book helps fill that void and inspires us all to put our hearts into whatever work we are focused on, as he always did.

John A. Burgener (Jr.)

MUSING ON HOW I LIVED SO LONG

Some people have asked me, "What is the secret of a long life?" I do not know. I have lived a reasonably healthy life. In fact, I drink alcohol in moderation, and I found smoking to be relaxing.

I used to close the door to my office and smoke a cigar after lunch. I considered that my quiet time and would not engage in any business during this break. I have smoked a pipe and a few cigars in the last 50 years. I also used to smoke on long car trips. I rarely smoked anywhere else. However, both my wife and my secretary objected to my cigar smoking. As Elinor was refusing to go on trips because of the smoking and my secretary was threatening to quit, I quit. Maybe smoking during stressful times and the cessation of smoking in less stressful times explains my old age.

I never was one to do physical exercises. The majority of my physical activity came from work projects like building a house, a cottage, and finishing the basement in every house we lived in. I built the original spectrograph and the equipment for my lab. I built a travel trailer. I kept busy on various other projects for the business and at home.

I really think it is up to God. God wants me to write some books and keeps me alive until I have done what he wants.

A birthday card from my son, Paul, has a button that I am entitled to wear that sums it up, "I have survived damn near everything."

MUSINGS ON MY LIFE

I had the great fortune of having active and resourceful parents. As a result, I have many memories of things we did that others never get the chance to do.

My earliest memory was the bravery of my mother. It was when we lived on Neville Park Avenue in the Beaches area in Toronto. I must have been about four years old. My father was out of town on business, and Uncle John, my mother's brother, had come for supper. As he was leaving after supper, he noticed that there was some activity on the street and, since my father was out of town, wondered if my mother wanted him to stay overnight. I clearly remember this because I had heard someone on our back porch and Uncle John's comment frightened me. My mother said she was all right and my uncle left.

I was put to bed, but some time later I heard a great crash. I ran into my mother's bedroom as she was running down the stairs. Her bedroom window was smashed. She phoned someone, then came back upstairs and told me to go to bed.

It seems she was preparing to go to bed when a man, standing on the veranda roof, ordered her at gunpoint to open her window. She apparently walked to the window, picked up a flowerpot from the table in front of the window (which she would have had to have done to open it), and threw it through the window, catching the burglar off-guard, causing him to lose his balance and fall off the porch roof. The police arrived a few minutes later and found the thief unconscious on the ground.

Apparently, a gang of thieves were robbing the street, so the police were already patrolling it. They praised my mother for her bravery and said they had one of the thieves in custody because of her action. Afterwards, my father installed a siren on our rooftop with a control switch beside the bed. He did this on all subsequent houses.

My mother actually risked her life to do what is right. If the thief had not fallen off the roof, he may well have shot my mother. Yielding to thieves is more common than fighting them. Fighting them can lead to personal harm, but it's what makes our society so good—that people are willing to stand up for their rights and take risks to ensure our rights. The modern-day concept that rights entitle us to a joyful life with no need for personal effort is nonsense—we only have rights that we are willing to fight for and take risks to keep.

The next memory was when we lived near my grandfather Burgener's factory in Sebringville, Ontario. My grandfather had some sickness and my father went to run the cheese factory. I believe we were there about a year. My brother Ernie was born while we were living there, so I must have been about five years old. The factory property was about one hundred acres with a river running through it called the Black Creek. My grandfather would take me hunting and fishing as he convalesced. He left a Swiss rifle to me in his will that we used when hunting. Sadly, I lost it several years later, while living in Lorne Park. A thief broke into the house and stole it. I actually saw the thief with my rifle the next week, and I accused him of stealing it. His answer was to load a bullet and point it at me and say, "Try to take it." I didn't. I told my father, and he said, "They are a rough family and if we go to the police, they will probably burn our house down or other action."

I remember the big steam engine that powered the factory, with all the belts and pulleys—electric motors were not available. Farmers drove their wagons, pulled by big horses with hairy legs, to empty their milk cans into a trough that led to large tanks where some liquid was added and the milk would curdle. The curds were removed, pressed in big cylinders to remove the whey, and then moved to the storeroom. My grandfather would check the maturity of the cheese by drawing a little cylinder of cheese and tasting it. He sometimes even asked me for my opinion. I really enjoyed spending time at the factory and with my grandfather.

When we moved back to the Toronto area, my parents bought a plot of land in Scarborough and built a temporary house to live in until a permanent house could be built. This was next door to my mother's sister Nellie, her husband Eddy Moldy, and my cousin Jack.

The most memorable event while living there was when I started school. I walked ten minutes to the Scarborough radial car, took it to the end of the line, and then hopped on a Kingston Road streetcar to the stop at the school. I also remember being hoisted over the side of a footbridge by two older boys and was left hanging. I finally let go and fell to the stream below, spraining both ankles, and had to crawl home.

The most serious event was the house fire. My father had bought new side curtains for our car and gave me a sheet of the clear plastic (celluloid) to play with. My mother had put us to bed for our afternoon rest. Our temporary quarters were a two-room house having a kitchen/living room and a bedroom with a stove near the door to the two rooms. I had put my celluloid sheet near the stove. It suddenly exploded, scattering burning celluloid all over the bedroom with a major fire at the stove. My mother ran through the flames and her hair caught fire. She grabbed a blanket to put out the burning hair. With the blanket on her back, she grabbed the baby and, standing in the doorway, ordered us to run past her and out of the house. She then went back in and put out the fire. We did not have a telephone to alert Dad, so when he came home, he found the house a mess and my mother cleaning up. My mother had some serious burns, but we children had none. I think the fire broke my parent's spirit as my next memory was living in a rented house near St. John's School.

Again, my mother risked herself to save us. She had the wisdom to think of how to get us out safely, but still personally got hurt in the process. So same comment as before—taking risks and accepting personal harm is necessary to survive.

There was an earthquake when we lived in a duplex on Bingham Street (I think) off Kingston Road. My parents had gone shopping and left me in charge; I was about seven-and-a-half years old. Suddenly, the house started shaking and a picture fell off the wall. I was starting to get my brother and sisters to run out of the house when my parents came in the door. I do not remember any aftershocks.

I remember living on the Lakeshore at the foot of Lee Avenue. On my first communion day, the family rode home in Dad's car with the top down; the sun was shining, and I was feeling great joy.

I also remember being beaten up by two older girls, who broke my front tooth by bashing my face against a fence. I remember the terrible pain as the dentist removed the tooth's nerve. The broken tooth later had to be removed, and I still have a missing front tooth.

I received a Meccano set when I was about seven years old. I added to it and, later on, even made gadgets for my business with it. I remember joining the choir and singing at Mass. Later, I was asked to join the senior choir and sing the Latin High Mass. I enjoyed singing the Mass.

I remember the first family camping trip to Rice Lake, where I was introduced to bloodsuckers. I went to the lake several times with my father to go fishing. We would leave home at what seemed to me to be the middle of the night so we could get an early start. I do not remember any great catches and I never became a fisherman, although I always enjoyed being with my father. Fishing seemed to be a rather dull pastime—sitting in a boat for hours to catch maybe a fish or two.

I also remember my father buying a Buick that had been in an accident. He stripped it down to its frame to make a base for a house trailer that he built and in which we used to go camping. One wall of the trailer folded down and had a canvas top. This wall held a double-bed mattress and two single-bed mattresses attached. The other three family members slept in the eating area. It had running water from a tank in the ceiling and electric lights from a battery charged by the car. It was a lot more comfortable than a tent.

Since it was built on a car frame, it had four wheels and had to be steered when towed. Dad had worked out a system through test runs. The first time we used it to go camping, the steering system broke and the trailer swung side-to-side as we crawled along to a service station. We spent our first night at the garage that fixed it. We never had the chance to really enjoy the trailer because the Crash of 1929 occurred that fall.

My mother's brother, Peter, had a similar Buick to Dad's reclaimed one. Uncle Peter decided that the wrecked Buick had an engine in better condition than his, so we replaced his engine. Our house had a drive shed and small barn. The barn had a lift for storing hay in the loft. We used this lift to replace my uncle's engine. I was about twelve and participated in the building of the trailer and switching the engine.

Until I was about eleven, we lived on the lakefront. I remember my father and I sitting on the porch, watching lightning storms on the lake. And there was a ghost. It would appear to the weakest in the bedroom as staring eyes. It frightened my mother's father, an Irishman, who was staying with us. He occupied the front room on the third floor, which had a deck. He said on more than one occasion that he saw the door open and close, but my mother thought he was dreaming. The clincher was the night he went to his room and there was a heavy dresser pushed against the door on the inside of his bedroom. That was enough for him! He wouldn't even visit us after that.

It turned out that a single man, living next door, spent his nights wandering the neighbourhood. We had big trees that overhung the roof of the house. Apparently, he climbed onto our roof and then onto our third-floor porch. There was no lock on the porch door as we never thought anyone would try to enter from the third level. The ghost tried frightening my mother and she let out a scream. Dad woke up and saw a figure go out the door of their porch on the second floor. Dad rushed out and saw the ghost climbing down the tree. We locked all the doors after that and never saw the ghost again. My grandfather was not convinced.

When I started school, I quickly found that I could not see the writing on the blackboard and had to get glasses. I think the difficulty in seeing made me see school as a challenge. I actually did reasonably well.

I think the sight problem also made me accept life as a challenge. Because of my poor sight, the sports I played were as much a challenge as fun. I always tended to pick amusements that were challenging and accomplished something. My father encouraged this by giving me more challenges. Instead of buying me skis, Dad bought hickory 2x4s for me to make my own skis and skis for my siblings. My homemade skis eventually wore out many years later during my working days in Arvida.

I enjoyed making things, like a model airplane with ribbed wings and an alcohol engine. At twelve, I built a radio. At fifteen, I salvaged and rebuilt a Ford Model T truck from a farmer's field and converted it to a hot rod. I eventually traded it in for a burned-out Chevrolet, which I later converted to a tractor.

In October 1929, I was twelve-and-a-half years old and the Great Depression of the thirties started. By the spring of 1930, it was apparent that the Depression was going to be severe and probably last for years. My parents decided to buy a piece of land big enough to feed our family of five children. They bought a 2-acre plot with fruit trees and a very basic house in Lorne Park (20 miles west of Toronto). In his spare time, during the summer of 1930, Dad began adding to the original three-room house. By September, it was ready to move into, in time for school.

So we moved from our nice house in the Beaches area of Toronto to our minimalist house in Lorne Park. I personally enjoyed it. The lack of facilities was of less concern than the advantages of living in the country. There was no running water; it had to be pumped at the well. The toilet was an outhouse. By the third year, Dad had added running water and a flush toilet, and it became a comfortable house. I was old enough to help do these improvements, getting experience others never received.

The school was a four-room school: Lorne Park Public School. Since we had come from a Catholic school, the principal insisted that we all go back at least one grade.

My parents objected. The other three teachers, who taught up to Grade 6, pointed out that each classroom covered two grades and there would not be a problem. The principal, who had been teaching at Lorne Park for 40 years, insisted that she would not submit my name to write the Grade 8 high school entrance examination. This did not sit well with me to have to spend at least one and perhaps two more years in elementary school. My parents arranged with Corpus Christi School, the previous Toronto school we had attended, to send lessons. From Easter on, I lived with Conrad Myers and attended Corpus Christi. I passed the entrance test with honours. When the principal was told of my accomplishment, her comment was, "Money can do anything."

My sisters and brother were all in lower grades and therefore were not affected by the principal's religious bigotry. However, when my sister, Marie, moved into Grade 8, she was at the mercy of the principal.

For the 1932–1933 school year, my parents rented an apartment near St. Basil's School, which was also close to St. Michael's College School, where I had started high school. The family moved into Toronto for the school year, thus eliminating the problem at Lorne Park.

In 1933, I turned 16 and Dad bought me a car. For the '33–'34 school year, my father drove us to school at St. Basil's, and I drove home. By '34–'35, the principal at Lorne Park had been replaced due to the efforts of my father. He worked to replace the school board and the new board fired the principal. We had no further problems at the school.

My father first bought me a Model T Ford, but it could not stand the 50-mile-per-day commute and was always causing trouble, so he bought me a 1927 Chevy that stood up to the daily grind. Not many parents would go to such lengths for the good of their children.

My father let me keep the car on the condition that I maintained it—not have a mechanic service it. I put the car to good use that fall by packing fruit not needed by the family into 6-quart baskets. With my brother Ernie's help, we loaded up my Chevy and a two-wheeled trailer and sold the produce door-to-door in Toronto for 25 cents. This income helped pay my tuition at St. Mike's and gave Ernie spending money. Ernie did so well that while still in high school he bought a 1928 Model A Ford—the first year Ford made a real car.

Always looking for a challenge and things to do made my life interesting and challenging. When I decided to go to university, I chose the most challenging science course offered. Since I was about to spend time and money, I wanted to get the most I could. It was a real tough course—only two graduated and I was one of the two.

Upon graduating in the spring of 1941, the middle of WWII, I was effectively drafted to improve the quality control in aluminum production vital for building fighter planes. I improved quality control from an 8-hour turnaround time to 30 minutes, which resulted in major changes in the production of aluminum. At the end of the war, I turned down an offer of a senior management position. In praying for guidance, I became aware that spending my life making aluminum was not challenging enough, and I could do more by starting my own laboratory.

In the fall of 1947, I left the Aluminum Company to start my own laboratory. When starting this, my wife Elinor and I lived with my parents while I built my spectrograph and accessories, saving the cost of buying a new spectrograph worth $70,000. We needed a house, but we did not have the down payment and rentals were in short supply due to the war. We managed to rent a shack with outdoor plumbing. With God's help, I overcame the difficulties of financing with no job, raising a family, starting a business, and physically building a house.

University &
Post-University Days

I often muse on my decision to go to university—as it changed my life—and how God directed me to do it.

I had hoped to win a scholarship but did not succeed, so I felt I did not have university-level ability. It was during the Depression and money was hard to come by. I was lucky and landed a job as a shipping clerk. Not many high school graduates found jobs in those days. There were no forklifts, so I learned to carry 100 kg bags of chemicals, but did very little else. The chemists and engineers had much better jobs than me, so I decided that if I did not want to spend my life carrying 100 kg bags of chemicals, I had better get a university degree.

In my spare time, I started to experiment with engines for watercraft. I wondered, why not use the gasoline explosion directly on the water? To test it, I built an engine consisting of a 2-inch pipe with a bend at 90 degrees. At the top end, I attached a valve and a spark plug. I used an electric motor to control the valve and spark plug, and bellows to inject the explosion mixture. The first test was performed in air with the pipe clamped in a vise. It operated well with a discharge once every 30 seconds. I then mounted the engine in a laundry tub and started up the engine. The first explosion was fine, but the backwash wet the spark plug, causing the subsequent explosion mixture to float on top of the water, and it suddenly ignited. Fortunately, I was using very small amounts of gasoline.

I decided that it needed more experimenting. I needed to find a way to let the exhaust gases escape and keep the spark plug dry. I tried various modifications and came up with one that I expected would overcome the difficulties. I set it up in the vice on the workbench and ran it with small amounts of gasoline and one minute between explosions. It worked well. So I increased the charge and set it to fire every 15 seconds. A huge flame shot out of the open end, and the bench shuddered on each explosion. I reached over to shut it off, but it broke out of the vice, sliding along the bench and spilling gasoline, resulting in a fire. Fortunately, I had attached a hose and immediately turned on the water, putting out the fire. My mother was entertaining her bridge club and complained about the smell of gasoline (not being aware of the fires). When my father came home, he discovered what had happened and suggested that further experiments be done together and not in the house.

We realized that we had an engine that worked directly without any auxiliary equipment—a jet engine. We did a few more tests and applied for a patent. That was 1936, some years before jets appeared. By then, university was starting, and I had no more time to experiment. If I had not gone to university, I would have continued the development of the jet engine and would probably be a multi-millionaire.

Since I had worked a year and saved every penny I could, I had the necessary funds for first year but would have to depend on earning enough for subsequent years. I decided I should at least see what the university had to offer. I obtained a University of Toronto calendar that described the courses offered. While sitting in a barbershop, waiting for my turn, I was thumbing through the calendar and happened to open it to the section on the mathematics and physics group of honour courses. The preamble mentioned that these courses were the most advanced science courses offered. The requirements to enter the program were stiffer than the other courses and required an honours level in high school at graduation. I had achieved honours in graduating but had not won a scholarship, yet I felt confident that I would meet the requirements.

At that moment, I somehow knew that I should consider these courses. Before the barber called me, I had firmly decided that physics and chemistry was the course I should take. I had been praying hard that I would take the courses God wanted me to take. Somehow I knew that physics and chemistry were the courses I should take. And when I look back, this was God telling me what to take.

That fall, I registered in the program and was told by the dean of mathematics that the course was too difficult for me, particularly the P&C option as it was both the complete honours physics and complete honours chemistry courses. He pointed out that this program required up to 40 hours a week in labs and lectures. In a further attempt to dissuade me, he indicated that the 44 students registered had all won scholarships, and I should select an easier program. I told him that I intended to take the courses and graduate. He replied that he admired my determination, but I was a fool. (I met him walking down Bay Street 15 years after I had graduated, and he recognized me. I must have impressed him.)

The first year was a common year for all the mathematics and physics courses; specialization came in second year. In physics and chemistry, there were 14 students in second year. By fourth year, there were three students, two of whom graduated—I was one of the two. Needless to say, I did a great deal of praying and studying. With God's help, I graduated.

It was a tough course. If there were times I doubted, I still knew on a fundamental level that I would make it if I didn't give up. There were many instances in my life when I knew that things would work out. In every case, I had prayed prior to the decision I made, and the action I should take was made known, sometimes by circumstances and other times by just knowing what I should do. God speaks to us in many ways.

The summer after first year, I accepted a summer job as a bellhop at the Royal Canadian Yacht Club on the Toronto Islands. The pay was $30 per month with room and board, and I expected there would be lots of tips. It turned out there was a no-tipping rule. Instead, there was a collection for the staff at the end of the season. This meant that my total earnings would be $90 plus whatever the year-end collection would bring (being a bellhop, my share would probably be a very small part of the collection). So I quit. But this put me behind in getting summer employment.

School tuition was $300, with expenses adding up to about $200 while living at home. That summer, I only made a total $300, so I went to see the registrar of St. Mike's and said I would have to postpone my return for second year in order to earn enough money. He asked me how much I had, and I told him. He told me to register for second year and St. Mike's would cover the university fees. Because of the generosity of St. Mike's, I was able to continue my education. Ever since graduation, I have contributed to St. Mike's so that they might do the same for other students.

Between second and third year, I worked at several jobs: driving a truck for six weeks, cleaning up after a fire, and working at a drive-in in Etobicoke from 8 p.m. until 2 a.m. I made enough to cover all my expenses. Between third and fourth year, I landed a contract to build an exhibit for the CNE as well as a contract to build PA amplifiers. I made over $1,000 that summer. I was rich beyond my wildest dreams and could even afford to take a girl on a date. Previous dates were always canoeing or some activity that cost little or nothing.

The family moved back to Toronto from Lorne Park because my sister did not think the pickings for a husband were very good in Lorne Park. My parents rented a big house on Edgewood Avenue in the Beaches area, which suited me as I had graduated from high school and had a job in Toronto in the Bay and College area. The house had a stairway from the kitchen to a room at the back of the house. I used this room as my study and workshop.

My sisters had frequent parties, some of which I also attended. During one such party, I was working on my ear exhibit and had no time to attend. My sister Jennie had invited her boyfriend and his sister Elinor. Some of the guests asked where I was, and my sisters answered that I was working on my ear. Elinor asked Jennie what was wrong with my ear, so Jennie brought Elinor up to see. Elinor was a member of the anti-communist association, the Social Forum, to which I belonged. I thought of her as just one of the girls. This time was different. She was dressed beautifully and with her light red hair, looked stunning. I saw her as the beauty she was for the first time. Jennie could have told her that I was working on an exhibit, but she had worded it in such a way that Elinor was especially intrigued.

Elinor had to have her tonsils removed and ended up in Toronto General Hospital a few blocks from the university. Since she was a member of the Social Forum, I felt it was my duty to visit her in the hospital. It was a most enjoyable visit. So when she ended up in the General Hospital again some months later due to a toboggan accident in which she was the only one hurt, I visited her each of the 10 days she was there and enjoyed it.

After the hospital, although I was in my last year at university and had very little spare time, I found time to visit with her. The Social Forum had a New Year's Eve party, and I invited Elinor. At the end of the party, I attended New Year's Day Mass at 12 a.m. at the cathedral and proudly escorted Elinor—still on crutches. Later that year, in the spring of 1941, I graduated from university and went to live in Arvida in northern Quebec, eight hundred miles from Elinor.

One did not find girlfriends in Arvida. The town supported the war industry, an air force base, a large army base, and thousands of construction workers expanding the plant and building the largest electric generating plant and dam in the world at that time. There were nine single men for every single woman. The unmarried technical staff lived in the Saguenay Inn, a beautiful inn where parties were held every week attended by the married residents of the area. But if you could find a girl, the young technical staff also attended. Usually, if you went to a Saturday night dance, there was one girl for at least half a dozen men.

At one of these parties, I was looking after the arrangements and therefore had no date. At about 10 o'clock, I was finished and went onto the dance floor. I saw a petite girl, dressed beautifully in white, who looked absolutely ravishing sitting there. I went over to ask her if she would like to dance. She accepted, and we danced the rest of the evening. I found out that her name was Peggy, and she was a teacher living in Kénogami, 10 miles away. Her escort became drunk, and she did not want anything to do with him. I offered to escort her home, but she felt that since I would have to hire a taxi, it was an imposition. I did not think so. However, another chap dating a girl from Kénogami also had to take a taxi, so we joined the other two, and I did escort her home. For the next several weeks, she accompanied me to the parties at the inn. She was a very nice person, and I really enjoyed our dates. After the third date, she wanted me to meet her family, which I did. Her father was a chief engineer working for the pulp and paper factory in Kénogami. I still had Elinor in mind and was not in a hurry to get married. However, Peggy was very pretty and vivacious. I expect she would have made a good wife.

Suddenly, on a Friday afternoon, I was advised that the equipment for the Kingston lab was in and I should be in Kingston Monday morning to set it up. The use of the spectrograph in Kingston was questioned by others since no one had ever used the spectrograph on concentrations above 5%; Kingston had alloys of 15%. I had assured my superiors it could be done, as some tests had demonstrated. The whole set-up was purchased on my assurance that I could do it. It was an important challenge that I had to deliver on within a three-month timeframe. So I left Arvida in a hurry on Saturday, without telling anyone, including Peggy. Apparently, others thought I had been transferred and left for good.

For the first couple of weeks, I lived in a hotel since I was working night and day to get things started. After that, I found a boarding house with a very nice couple who had a daughter my age. She was a beauty and a very nice person. She invited me out to a couple of plays, but I worked almost every night, so really I saw very little of her.

Besides setting up and training staff, I had to develop procedures to use the equipment. I developed the spectrochemical procedures in ranges that at that time were considered outside the range of spectrochemistry. Living in Kingston for three months made it possible for me to go home on weekends when I was not working.

When I returned to Arvida from Kingston, it was the end of December 1942. I found out Peggy was engaged to an air force officer. If Peggy had been available when I returned, she might have been competition for Elinor. If Peggy had known I was gone for three months, she might have waited, but again the hand of God made it apparent that Elinor was to be my wife. The timing of Elinor's tonsillectomy, her 10-day stay in hospital after the toboggan accident, the months on crutches, and trips home on the weekends over three months, gave me the opportunity to see Elinor. Peggy was in too much of a hurry for marriage.

These circumstances were all directed to cause Elinor to be my wife. Every indication was that God wanted me to marry Elinor, and I did on September 11, 1943. I thank God for directing me so. We spent three good years in Arvida.

I treasure the memory of our first Christmas as we walked home from midnight Mass at 40 below zero, the snow crunching with each step. The northern lights danced in the sky. My heart was filled with love for Elinor and I thanked God for her and such beauty.

The last year in Arvida, things were unsettled. The company invited 75 of the top employees to a meeting and said that with the end of the war they would have to downsize, but everyone present was guaranteed a job.

Two months later, 25 of those attending the meeting were let go. The company wanted to pick the ones to go because the better employees were leaving and they could easily find jobs. That annoyed me. The company sold our house to our neighbour, who became a miserable landlord. I spent my holidays looking into job possibilities and actually received an offer from Cornell University, but did not want to live in the States.

Munroe Fraser, who worked in Arvida, owned the Fraser Industrial Hardware in Galt through his father. He offered to help finance me if I started my own spectrochemical business. I enquired about dealerships of spectrographic equipment suppliers and Jarrell Ash offered 10% on any sales I made in Canada.

After much prayer, Elinor and I decided that if the company transferred me to the Alulabs Research Labs in Kingston, Ontario, as I was already on the Alulabs payroll, we would stay with the company. Otherwise, we would set up our own business. I approached the company, but they refused, saying that the research facilities were better in Arvida and they could not use me in Kingston. I decided to leave and gave the company a couple months' notice. I hoped they would be a customer.

Dr. Hainey, who I had met when in Kingston and had taken me out to lunch, was the director of research for Aluminum Limited—the holding company of Alcan. In the last two weeks before our departure, he came to Arvida and offered me a three-year training program in Switzerland with all expenses paid and a guarantee that at the end of the course I would be given a senior management position. Thanking him, I pointed out that if they had made this offer two months earlier, I probably would have accepted it. In my praying, it had become apparent to me that by staying with the company, I would spend my life making aluminum, and I felt I could do more with my life than make aluminum. I might have had an economically richer life, but not a better life.

Our Family

When I think of Elinor, my loving and beautiful wife, I realize how fortunate I was to marry her. We loved one another and were married for 68 years. We had a good marriage based on a firm belief in God and with God's help, we raised four children. In our marriage, the family was prime.

Elinor recognized that our most important job was raising our children. She set the tone of our family, making sure that our children grew up as good, kind, holy, and useful adults. She was the perfect wife for me and a wonderful mother.

When I look back on those days at the start of my business, they were difficult, yet Elinor never complained. We agreed that Elinor would stay at home looking after the children and being present to them whenever the need arose. Elinor could easily have been employed outside the home in a good, well-paying job. In Arvida, she was the second-highest-paid secretary. In the early days of our own business, it would have made things financially easier if Elinor had had a job. But Paul was a child and Peter was born soon after we moved into our partly finished house.

From the autumn of 1947 to the late summer of 1951, we had very little income and lived mainly on the meagre savings we had and the mortgage money that we drew on as our house was being completed. When Peter was born in May 1950, we did not have the money to release Elinor and Peter from the hospital. Those were the days before OHIP and the hospital would not sign you out until the bill was paid. Fortunately, a client paid their bill and I had enough to pay the hospital bill. This was on top of owing the lumber companies a lot of money for the house construction.

Not only did Elinor not complain, but she also encouraged me. She went along with all the hardships of having no money, living in a shack for a year with outdoor plumbing, then living in a partly built house with no kitchen cupboards, a plywood counter for the sink, and lumber stacked all over the house. After Peter's birth, she acquired an infection and was quite sick. Her mother and my mother came to look after the children and Elinor. They both spent a lot of time telling her what a fool she was to put up with the life I was forcing her to live because of my dream. Added to this, I had an offer of a good job as a research director at Guelph University. Elinor's answer was, "He is my husband and I know what he is doing will be for the best." I thanked her and still thank her because few women, if any, would have put up with it.

The lumber company had a lot of customers like me with outstanding bills, and the bank took over. The bank sent a bully to frighten the debtors. The neighbours next door were also building. The bank frightened them into an unfavourable second mortgage. The bank representative yelled at Elinor and threatened to send in a bailiff and take over our house. I arranged to meet him and pointed out that he could not foreclose on our house since the mortgage company would have priority. Further, he could sue me, but I would acknowledge the debt and offer to pay $10 a month. There was a good chance the court, because of my present economic conditions, would agree. Or, he could approve the $1,500 of additional lumber I needed to finish the house and get my final mortgage payment and pay off my debts. He then demanded a guarantor, but I pointed out that with a guarantor, I could get lumber from other sources. He finally agreed that if my father would guarantee $800 (half the amount owing), he would authorize the $1,500 of additional lumber. We were desperate for money. But I never considered having Elinor work outside the home. I guess I depended on God. I believed that God directed me to start my own business and I expected that God would eventually solve it. He did.

In the summer of 1951, I earned $10,000 by selling a complete lab to the Geological Survey of Canada—that was a lot of money in those days. Added to this, the laboratory business was producing an income. We had money when John was born, in the fall of 1951, to release him from the hospital. The total cost of building the house was $6,000, plus my labour. The amount of the first mortgage that I secured was $5,800, plus a government second mortgage of $2,000. Labour costs in house building were estimated at 50%. With the final mortgage draw and the sale commission, we could pay all our debts and improve our standard of living. I could never have done it without Elinor's help.

If we had done as our mothers had demanded and I accepted the job in Guelph, we would have had a good middle-class life. We would have had a nice house, probably visited Europe once, and maybe taken a cruise somewhere. But because of our perseverance, Elinor had seven trips to Europe, fifteen cruises, lived in five-bedroom houses in exclusive areas, and I changed the way the world practices analytical chemistry. I think Elinor would agree it was worth it.

Raising Children

Our children became exceptional adults and this is because Elinor considered raising children a full-time activity that needed a mother and a father. The objective was to develop a good adult. Any activity that did not lead to a good adult was not permitted. Activities that led to kindness, thoughtfulness, determination, interest in learning, and holiness were encouraged. Such habits need to be reinforced constantly. A child needs to be directed and assisted to accomplish and embrace these habits. This is not an activity that can be accomplished in the parents' spare time.

Children not only have physical needs, but their spiritual and intellectual needs have to be satisfied as well. The spiritual needs include the development of personality and behaviour to produce an intelligent, loveable, and holy adult who will be an asset to humanity. Parents must also act according to their objectives. Elinor and I believed that activities that were cute or funny, selfish or demanding, if not contributing to a good adult, were not to be encouraged or permitted.

When our son Paul was a little over two years old, he started to exhibit what appeared to be convulsions. Every time he had a convulsion, a great fuss was made over him. Upon taking him to the doctor, Paul was diagnosed with infected tonsils and it was recommended that they be removed. About a month after the operation, Paul suddenly developed convulsions again. I noticed that now when he had a convulsion, he was alert and his eyes were watching us. We consulted with the doctor, and he indicated that there was no reason for a convulsion. The next time this happened, I grabbed Paul, rushed him upstairs, dropped him in his crib, and walked out of the room. He never had another convulsion.

Children can be smart and quickly learn how to get attention. Parents have to recognize the tricks and be firm by not allowing the behaviour. We recognized that humans are spiritual beings, and that personality and behaviour are spiritual characteristics that need development and encouragement. I believe our children grew up happy because we had rules that they could understand and which made sense to them.

Religion played an important role in our marriage. We were both very active in our parish and were very concerned that our children should receive a very good grounding in religion. Our sons were altar boys and were encouraged to take part in church affairs. Family prayer was also encouraged. On long automobile trips, we said the rosary as we started on the trip. The house had pictures of the Sacred Heart, statues of the saints, and a crucifix at the entrance. We treated the home as a sanctified place where one could live in the presence of God. The children were taught to pray, attended Catholic schools, and went to Mass every Sunday, even when travelling.

Schooling was also very important. We rewarded good marks and made sure homework was done. They were all good students. We also believed that a segregated high school was desirable. Our sons went to Michael Power (a private Catholic boys' high school) and Debbie started at Holy Name of Mary (a private Catholic girls' high school). Debbie did not do well there, having been brought up with three brothers; she was out of place in a girls school and transferred to Lorne Park High School. Raising children is a long-term activity, needing a plan and the determination to carry it out.

We believed that intelligence has a lot to do with experience; therefore, we would give our children as many experiences as possible. We often went out for breakfast after Sunday Mass. We took the children to movies and other entertainments. Travelling is broadening and interesting. We made it a point to travel by automobile wherever possible as there was much more to see and experience than by train or airplane, although we did give them some experience of train and plane travel. On one occasion, we travelled to Ottawa by train, and I remember Peter suddenly standing up and pointing and saying, "There is a diesel engine"; at that time, diesel engines were just starting to replace steam engines.

By seeing how others live and the practices of different people, one recognizes that one's own way of living is not the only way. Other ways of life are certainly interesting and can be of value to the traveller. Travelling also gives a perspective on history. Seeing a picture of a medieval castle is interesting, but to actually visit such a castle makes history live and forces one to recognize that there was greatness in history. Similarly, to see a picture of the Canadian

Rockies or the Swiss Alps is interesting, but cannot give the sense of beauty and grandeur that a visit does. These are experiences that one cannot get from books.

We wanted the children to use their imagination, and travelling to very different destinations does excite the imagination. We took the children to Europe, driving through Holland, France, Italy, Switzerland, and Germany. In Switzerland, we visited the area where my father and grandfather were born. We also traversed the United States and Canada from coast to coast, as well as many visits to Florida. We often spent weekends camping and have camped in many areas of Ontario: Rondo on Lake Erie, Algonquin Park, Georgian Bay, Silver Lake. Camping encourages the acceptance of some minor inconveniences and self-reliance that hotels or resorts do not. Travelling broadens one, and we wished to raise children with a broad view and attitude to life. The children have become good and successful adults. They were happy children.

We also made it a practice to involve the children in as many family activities as possible, including travelling with me on business trips. As the children grew up and had their own families, we always had room for them to visit with their families. Until Elinor and I moved to a condo, we lived in five-bedroom houses and afterwards built a cottage—there was always room for visitors.

MEMORABLE
FAMILY TRIPS

I consider travelling for children broadening and believe it helps to improve the ability to imagine. One of the reasons to be in my own business was the ability to take my family on business trips.

I had some business family trips that were memorable. My first business trip to Europe was to London, England, to spend some time at Hilger & Watts, a supplier of quartz prism spectrographs. My company, Technical Service Laboratories (TSL), was a reseller of the Hilger & Watts equipment and they had offered me an increase in TSL's discount if I would spend some time at their factory to become more familiar with their line of equipment. That was the autumn of 1956. Flying to Europe was an adventure those days. One got dressed up to do so. The Malton Airport (now Toronto Airport) was a small wooden building with an observation deck on the roof. One walked out to the airplane and climbed up the steps. The cost of the return flight was $580. That spring I had bought a new top-of-the-line Dodge station wagon for $2,700. The $580 was the equivalent of $6,000 today. It shows how inflation has lowered the value of our money.

I decided I would make the trip also a holiday, so I included Elinor and Paul, who was still a child's half fare.

Peter and John were five and four. They stayed with Jim and Jennie.

I spent a week at Hilger's while Elinor and Paul enjoyed London and the surrounding country. In the evenings, I would go to places Elinor had found interesting. One evening, we decided to leave Paul in the hotel and we would go to night club. There was a billboard I passed on my way to Hilger's advertising Murray's Cabaret Club. So we decided to go. When the floor show started, there were nudes standing at the side, and the dancers were also almost nude. Elinor was shocked, but she was even more shocked when after the show the dancers remained dressed as they were in the show, even the nudes, and came out and sat with the customers.

At the end of the week, I rented a car, crossed the Channel on a ferry and spent two weeks travelling on the continent. The trip included a visit to Switzerland where my father was born, northern France, Germany, and Italy. Northern France and Germany were still in the rubble of the war. Many places were still devastated. Southern France was not war-torn. In Italy, there was much destruction, but a lot had been rebuilt.

In Munich, we again left Paul in the hotel, and we went to a beer garden. We expected that children would not be allowed. Germany has a different attitude and there were lots of children in the beer garden. When we decided to go back to the hotel, we could not remember its name. We had a moment of panic because we had left Paul there. Fortunately, I had parked my English car on the street in front of the hotel. So we took a taxi and ask him to drive around the downtown hotels to find a car with an English licence. After the third hotel, we saw our car. After that, I always took the name of the hotel where we stayed in writing. It was a great trip.

In 1957, we bought a travel trailer and went on a business trip to New Brunswick, where we sold an on-site laboratory to a mining development company. We then proceeded down to Maine, where we camped for a week on the ocean.

In 1958, I planned a sales trip to Western Canada and decided to make it a family trip by driving with the trailer across the USA and returning through Canada. We drove with the family through Chicago to Mount Rushmore and viewed the presidents carved on the mountain, to Yellowstone National Park, through the badlands to San Francisco, up the Pacific Coast to Vancouver, and back across Canada. We stopped in the Rockies, went north of Banff to the Columbia Icefield, then to Jasper National Park, and on to Edmonton, where I installed a spectrograph at the university. Then, we continued on to Regina, where I sold the RCMP a complete lab, followed by Saskatoon and Winnipeg, where I made calls but sold nothing. After spending a very cold night in Winnipeg, we drove home.

In 1959, I did another business trip to Eastern Canada. This trip, we made a sale to the RCMP at Sackville, NB, and visited a mining site in Nova Scotia that resulted in a research program. We visited The Magnetic Hill and stayed in a park on the Bay of Fundy and then took the ferry to Prince Edward Island. We returned home through

Maine, New Hampshire, and Vermont, crossing back to Canada at Brockville.

In 1961, we made another family business trip. This time I had to go to England, Sweden, and France. So I arranged for Elinor to fly to London with Peter, John, and Debbie. We left Paul at home, since he was in his final high school year. We arranged that Elinor and the kids would arrive in London when I expected to be finished. I would meet her there and we would all fly to Paris, where we would rent a car and spend two weeks travelling in Europe.

When I got to England, arrangements had been made for me to go to Holland. This completely upset my schedule, and I was not able to meet Elinor in London. So I wired her that I would meet her in Amsterdam, and arranged for the people in London to meet her on arrival and to take her to a hotel and arrange her flight to Amsterdam. However, I then had to go to Sweden and expected to be back in Amsterdam two days after she arrived. Sweden proved to be a longer trip than expected. So Elinor was in Amsterdam for ten days. I finally got to Paris, where I had a day's work, and phoned her and said I would fly to Amsterdam the next day. She said she preferred to fly to Paris that night as she was running out of money. I arranged a flight that evening and met her at last. We rented a car the next day and started on our holiday. The boys enjoyed it. Debbie was only four years old and did comment that she would sooner be playing with Janet instead of visiting castles.

The School System

In my day, classroom sizes were made up of 35 to 40 students. We learned more than the 20 students currently in classrooms. I have grandchildren who, in Grade 8, could hardly write and had difficulty reading. They were not slow learners; they have done very well in business.

During the Depression, a teacher was glad to have a job. Teachers did not belong to unions, which today encourage teachers to demand more and do less so the unions can have more dues. I also blame the ineffectiveness of today's teaching on the rule that the teachers cannot discipline a student and must pass them to the next grade, whether they are ready or not.

BULLYING

We had bullies in my youth. I expect bullying has always been around. Growing up, it was not considered too serious. In general, we were taught to ignore it or, if it became too annoying, to fight back. I recall three outstanding bullies.

At Corpus Christi School, Conrad Myers, a black boy, was constantly bullied. I often took his part when some mean kid would start bullying him. As a result, we became close friends and that friendship lasted all our lives. He died last year [2014] at 96.

There was a super bully at the school. He would walk up to someone, punch the person in both eyes and walk away. Nothing was ever done about it. He did the same to me. He walked up to me, pulled my glasses off, stomped on them, and then punched me in both eyes. Since he had broken my glasses, this made it more serious and my parents complained. The police were called, but nothing happened. A month or so later he did the same to my sister, Marie.

My dad said we needed a weapon to protect ourselves. He gave us each a big heavy pencil box and said, "If this guy approaches one of you, start bashing him with the pencil box. Don't wait for him to do anything." A week or so later, he approached Marie and she did as Dad had instructed—she started bashing him with her pencil box.

He left her alone and never attacked Marie or me again. The bully needs to be bullied, because he thinks it is fun. If he is bullied, he discovers it is not fun.

Another bully used to harass me as I walked home from school. He was supported by his older brother. They would push me around, grab my books, and throw them in the mud or some other annoying action. Of course, when I arrived home, I was condemned for being so careless with my books. This went on for a whole school year. Come the summer, I was relieved because these bullies did not frequent the places I did. The reprieve was not to last as they started up again. This time I had had enough, I saw red and sailed into them by punching and kicking—anything I could do. They turned and ran. Oddly enough, we became friends.

In high school, one bully liked to get others into trouble. One of his tricks was to grab your books and throw them out a window so you did not have your homework to show to the teacher and received a deten-tion. He also did this to me. The trick that really angered me occurred when I had driven to school and parked my car on the sloping driveway. I had not locked the car. The culprit let the handbrake off and pushed the car down the driveway where it backed onto a main street, potentially causing a serious accident. Fortunately, I happened to be nearby and jumped into the car and stopped it. He stood there, laughing.

At the end of the next class, he made fun of the event. I walked up to him, very angry, and he punched at me. I had been learning jujitsu, so when he punched at me,

JOHN E. BURGENER

I grabbed his arm and, with a jujitsu manoeuvre, threw him over my shoulder, landing him on his back over a desk. I was terrified that I had broken his back. He got up, walked to his seat, and went home after the next class. He did not return for three days. Every day, I expected the police to come and arrest me. They never came, and when he returned to school, he said nothing. No one messed with me after that. He stopped his bullying and became a friend.

I believe the best treatment for a bully is to bully the bully and make him realize that the bullying is not fun.

LIFE AS IT WAS

Growing up, life moved at a slower pace. The horse and wagon were more plentiful than automobiles. Very few people had a car, so stores and services had delivery staff. The deliveries were made by horse-drawn wagons. One commonly saw the milkman, the bread man, the mailman, the iceman, the coalman, the Simpson's man, and the Eaton's man. All of these services have disappeared. The milkman delivered milk every day. The bread man and iceman delivered twice a week. In general, we children knew the delivery men and they, in turn, knew the children. It was a friendlier world. Children would follow the iceman, hoping to get a piece of ice to suck. The coalman, whenever you needed coal, came by horse-drawn wagon and carried the big bags of coal on his back to your coal chute. An opening on the side of your house led into the basement coal bin. I had to count the bags and tell my mother before she would pay him. As the automobile became more commonplace, the remaining delivery services used trucks. The milkman and the iceman still used horses and, except for the mailman, were the last to go. The mailman walked, but in recent years is using a truck and even that is now coming to an end.

I used to go to Saturday afternoon movies for 10 cents; they were child-oriented and ran a serial movie. Every week, they ended with the star being shot or falling off a cliff. The next week you found out that the main character survived. I'll never forget the first sound movies. You heard gunshots and car crashes, but no talking. Then the talkies, as we called them, became universal. Movie newsreels started showing events from all parts of the world. If an unusual event occurred, you went to the movies to see it. Today, while sitting in our living rooms, we see situations as they happen. The reason catastrophes seem to happen more frequently is that we instantly see everything happening. We only used to hear of developments in our immediate area and then only the most serious occurrences.

Adult streetcar tickets cost four for a quarter. Children's tickets, those up to eight years and whose height was determined by a mark on a pole beside the conductor, cost 16 for a quarter. Streetcar tickets for a student of any size were ten for a quarter with a student card. A Coke was a nickel and so was an ice cream cone. Bowl's Lunch had a special: a bacon and egg sandwich with a cup of coffee for 25 cents. (Dad and I often met for lunch at Bowl's in my high school days.) A good used car was $150. A monthly commuter train ticket from Toronto to Lorne Park (there was a station at Lorne Park) was $10. The cost of commuting was almost as high as the tuition at St. Michael's College High School.

We also did a lot more walking. Dad and I walked to and from Lorne Park station (a mile-and-a-half) through the farmers' fields, morning and evening.

From Union Station, I took a Bay Street streetcar north and disembarked two blocks south of Bloor Street. I usually arrived at the school five minutes before class, although I was frequently late and had to serve an automatic detention. It didn't bother me, since I had to wait until 5:20 p.m. for the train home. In fact, I often went to the detention room to do my homework. The person supervising the detention could not understand why anyone voluntarily went to detention. I never told them why. At other times, I would go to my father's office and find a desk to do my homework. After school, unless the weather was bad, I walked back to Union Station.

Since the school was a boarding school, we had no classes on Wednesday afternoon. To compensate for the hours missed, we had classes on Saturday morning. Twice a week, I took a 1:30 p.m. westbound train to Chicago that had a whistle stop at Port Credit. It was only supposed to stop there to pick up passengers, not let them off. The train would slow down as it approached Port Credit and, if no signal, speed up. I would jump off at Port Credit; the conductor would tell me when to jump. It was dangerous, but I was never hurt and learned the technique of jumping forward so that landings were in a running position. After the jump, I had a three-mile walk home. In bad weather, I would go to the museum for the afternoon and take the 5:20 p.m. train home. All this exercise in my teens probably contributed to my old age.

I had a car to take my siblings to school in Toronto when we were having trouble with the local Lorne Park school. After that, I rarely used it to go to school. On occasion, when my mother wanted to go shopping downtown, I would drive in and pick her up after school.

With gasoline at 30 cents a gallon (about three-and-a-half liters), it cost too much.

Cameras were available in my childhood, but certainly not as common as they are today. I have a couple of photographs from my childhood because my Uncle Chris, my father's brother, was a photographer. He roused my interest in photography. I can remember my uncle making colour prints by a colour separation process long before colour prints became available.

The box camera was a box with a lens and a shutter at one end and film on the other. There were no adjustments. You just took a picture. When the roll was full, you took it to the drug store to be developed. Movie film was available in Kodachrome and produced beautiful colour movies. I bought my first home movie camera in 1942. I was the only person I knew, or even met, who had a movie camera. I have taken thousands of feet of film, all in colour. At one time, people wanted to see my movies. Now the movie camera has been replaced by video cameras and, more recently, by any camera, including those on a cell phone.

The radio, television, and telephone have made huge advances. When I was about six, my father built a radio. We received stations as far away as Buffalo and Rochester, New York. Our neighbours would come to our house just to hear the radio and marvel at the great distances we could reach. I remember my father telling people that the ability to receive signals from such long distances was because he had built the latest design—a superheterodyne. The name stuck in my mind. At first, earphones were used, but then my father came home with a loudspeaker so that more people could listen to the radio at the same time. The radios were battery operated and used vacuum tubes—glass evacuated tubes that required a lot of energy to function. The radio needed a long wire to act as an antenna. By the time I reached high school, radios had become universal.

Another device my dad had built was a shortwave radio. He used Morse code to communicate and encouraged me to learn. I never became good at it, but could struggle along to send and receive messages. Morse code was soon forgotten by the general public as voice communication followed. Morse code is in limited use today; mostly in emergencies, since the code can be transmitted with simple equipment under poor transmission conditions and is independent of a person's voice.

Another great change was the telephone. The telephone had a crank on the side. To make a call, you turned the crank several times, an operator would ask you for the number you wanted, and she would connect you. Household phones were party lines of two or more families. In the countryside, there could be half a dozen households on one line. My father, in his early twenties, patented a system that made a party line act like a private line. Included in the patent was the mercury switch, which is used today in millions of thermostats. When Westinghouse started to produce his switch, he consulted a lawyer and was informed that his patent was weak and Westinghouse would spend millions of dollars defending themselves, so if he did not have millions to fight a lawsuit, he was better off to forget it, which he did. You can thank my father for the mercury switch in the thermostat in your house that controls your furnace or air conditioner.

My father spent his working life in the communication business. In his twenties, he formed a company called Signal Systems Limited. He provided call systems for hospitals and industry. He used bells or lights to signal personnel. When installing his system in St. Michael's Hospital, he frequently had to consult with Jennie Flynn in administration, and they fell in love and became my parents.

By the early 1920s, my father was running into competition with telephone companies and sold out to an intercom company. He sold, installed, and serviced Dictograph Executive Intercoms until he retired.

On weekends, I often helped my father service the executive systems. As a result, I have sat in the office chairs of many executives, such as the Premier of Ontario, and the presidents of major banks and industries. On one occasion, as I sat in the chair of a bank president, he came in. In the discussion that followed, he offered me a summer job as a handyman at his cottage. My father thought I should take the job because of the good contacts I would probably make, but contacts did not pay my tuition. I did not accept it as I could earn more at other summer jobs. I did learn a lot about servicing telephone systems. Since then, I have seen the changes in telephone communication up to the mobile and cell phones.

HOUSEKEEPING

As a teenager, my mother kept me busy doing household chores such as beating rugs and waxing and polishing floors. In my lifetime, I have seen a major change in housework due to advances in modern household equipment and improvements like iron-free clothes. Housekeeping chores have become less time-consuming than in earlier times.

I can remember my mother using a scrubbing board to wash clothes until we purchased our first washing machine—how pleased my mother was. Since there were no commercial detergents, mother used to make soap from fat and lye, which she used for house cleaning. She used flaked or powdered soap in the washing machine. Very dirty clothes still had to be hand scrubbed on the washboard. The washing machine did not spin dry the clothes, so each piece had to be put through the wringer individually. Once, my mother got her hair caught in the wringers. Fortunately, she had the presence of mind to press the safety release and no injury occurred.

I also remember our first vacuum cleaner. It relieved me of having to hang the rugs on the clothesline and beat them with a rug beater.

A great improvement was iron-free shirts. My mother ironed everything, even the bedsheets. Steam irons came into use in the early fifties. Before then, clothes had to be dampened before ironing. Many clothes had to be pressed under a damp ironing cloth. The clothes, after washing and going through the wringer, had to be pinned to a clothesline outside—summer and winter. In the winter, they froze stiff but, nevertheless, dried to a damp state.

The electric clothes dryer was a great improvement; that came some years after I was married. While Elinor and I lived in northern Quebec, I built a clothes dryer with an electric heater and fan, which was especially helpful to dry diapers in sub-zero weather. Every day there were diapers to wash and baby bottles to sterilize. Cloth diapers are rarely used now, having been replaced by disposable diapers and bottles are sterilized in the dishwasher.

Previously, food mixing was done with an egg beater or big spoon. Before electric refrigerators, one used an icebox. A block of ice was delivered to your house a couple of times a week. The kitchen stove was fuelled by coal, or wherever gas was available, a gas stove was used. The electric stove came into use in the thirties. Breakfast foods were Quaker Oats, Roman Meal, Corn Flakes or Shredded Wheat—not the huge selection of today.

We had electric lights when I was a child, although most farms and villages used coal oil lamps for light. Heat from a basement furnace was only available in the latest homes in the cities. Most homes, including our Lorne Park home, were heated with a stove located in the kitchen or with a Quebec heater in the living room. Coal or wood was used as fuel, which would often burn out during the night, making it a very cold house to wake up to in the morning. On those days, we did not go to school but stayed in bed until the house warmed up.

Eventually, my dad installed a hot water system for our Lorne Park house. It was easier to install water pipes in an already built house than hot air ducts. It served us well, and it made the second and following winters more comfortable. The hot water heating system also made it easier to expand as we added more rooms.

COMMUNICATION

When I consider the explosion of communication technologies today, I think of another period in history that opened with an information explosion—the invention of the printing press in 1440. Prior to the Gutenberg press, ideas and new ways of thinking were transmitted by word of mouth or were handwritten. Manuscripts were very valuable and often limited to only one copy. For example, Bible manuscripts were often chained in a church so that they could not be stolen.

Very few people ever had a reason to read; therefore, many people had only a very limited ability to read. So the possibility of the average person engaging in a learned discussion was also very limited. With the development of the press and its ability to spread information to many people, there was reason to be able to read and reading ability increased. Now it was possible for many people to read a report, a document, or a discussion by a writer in a different community. Ideas were more easily exchanged and could be printed many times and distributed over large areas. They could be circulated to hundreds of people with very little effort.

Explorers had been coming back with tales of wealth and wonders of the world since Grecian times, yet no great migration followed. The vast majority never heard the accounts. After the invention of the printing press, the stories of new lands, such as those in North America, were readily available. The great emigrations from Europe soon followed.

Less than one hundred years after the introduction of printing, Martin Luther spearheaded the great revolution in Christianity. Luther's ideas were easily spread. So were the ideas of those who read Luther's ideas. The Gutenberg press had changed the world.

New ideas are exciting. People love excitement. The Catholic Church, which had satisfied the religious needs of people for 1,500 years, was not exciting. So the new exciting religions that depended on the charisma of exciting leaders prospered. Over the centuries, the charisma of those leaders wore off, and many of the sects have disappeared or changed radically which, in itself, demonstrates that the new ideas were not necessarily founded on truth. The Reformation led to a new kind of intolerance, and hatred between the various sects was easily spread by the press.

The problem of wide and easy communication is that the ideas spread are not vetted in any way as to whether they are good or evil. Today, the press is being used to spread false information. For example, the fear of nuclear energy, the fear of climate change, the condemnation of oil sands development, and many other unfounded attitudes are spread by people who have limited knowledge in the field or who have an agenda. How many of those who condemn nuclear energy or the oil sands have actually studied nuclear energy and its risks, or visited the oil sands? Would any of them be able to critically evaluate the arguments for or against? Yet they firmly believe the media and other sources of criticism as relaying the truth. Although they are aware that the sources of information know as little as they, it is still published and supported. They continue the spread of information, whether it be true or false.

The young are consumed with the excitement of new technology and are easily persuaded to forget the old and unexciting. Truth is rarely exciting. So with the excitement of huge technological developments, it is essential that adults are able to pass on their wisdom. One can expect the young to readily accept the new attitudes and ideas without considering the reality or truth, and ignoring the old and established truths. Unfortunately, many adults have the wisdom of youth and are also consumed with technology. One wonders if this breakneck pace of technological change is good. In nature, change is very slow.

Technological advance does not increase wisdom. Because it becomes so absorbing, it may actually decrease wisdom. An increase in communication without a corresponding increase in wisdom opens the door to many evils like pornography, hate-mongering, and political unrest. It greatly enhances the opportunity to spread truth and spread untruth, which is always presented as truth. A hundred years ago, the youth heard their truth from parents and relatives. Today, they get what is supposed to be the truth from many sources, much of which is from those who have limited knowledge in the areas they are advocating. The information the young are acquiring is no longer controlled by the wisdom of their elders. Technology has thrown a burden on parents, and society as a whole, that they must learn to handle.

MARRIAGE TODAY

Our married life was a successful one, filled with love and included three children of our own and one adopted. We not only fulfilled God's purpose of marriage (to increase and multiply), but we also reaped the benefits of a good marriage through our four wonderful children, who have been a joy to us. Our experience is almost the exception today.

With widespread disinterest in God, marriage is not a commitment to one another in the presence of God, nor does it fulfil God's command to increase and multiply. Today, marriage is simply a legal contract, providing certain privileges and perhaps with the commitment to having no more than two offspring. Couples certainly are not putting their married life into the hands of God. Instead, they are telling God what He is to expect from them and, with abortion and contraception, they will see to it that it happens. How can such a marriage expect to have God's favour? Couples are not even fulfilling their civic duty to have a replacement level of children. Marriage, even without God, is a serious undertaking that in order to be successful, requires a serious commitment to each other to live as one. It is supposed to be for life, yet a large percentage of couples break up within five years.

A hundred years ago, the breakup of a marriage was not common. The majority of marriages were performed in a church by a minister and were recognized as being in the presence of God. Now, marriages are performed on a beach or in a park, thus diminishing the importance of marriage. It becomes a fun thing, not a life-changing action. God is left out, and couples do not expect God's help. They have to do it alone.

When Jesus told the apostles that marriage was for life, the apostles said that it was impossible. Jesus answered that it was impossible for man, but not for God. Marriages without God are not getting God's help.

I believe another cause of failure is the practice of living together before marriage. The argument is one can find out if the couple is compatible. Since there is no commitment, they cannot actually experience the committed life that marriage requires. If they do marry, they expect marriage to be an extension of the uncommitted life they led. Marriage is a committed life and those who live together are not prepared for the commitment. When times become difficult, as happens with any close relationship, they are not accustomed to commitment, so they break up. The personal independence reinforced while living together is still there. They are not accustomed to giving up their independence.

The availability of divorce also encourages a breakup. One does not have to become more tolerant; instead, one can have a divorce. Jesus' plan for marriage is a commitment of a man and a woman for life, requiring serious consideration worthy of an intelligent person with a free will. Such a marriage is better for society and for any offspring. The married couple become better persons by submitting to the good of their partner. The children, and society as a whole, benefit from a good, committed marriage.

There should be compulsory preparation courses before marriage. The Catholic Church demands that couples take pre-marriage courses. It is a very serious commitment. Divorce should only be possible in serious cases of abuse. Such preparation would allow the couple to seriously consider the difficulties marrying could bring. A good marriage is made in heaven. Unfortunately, many marriages are not viewed in this way.

Any other purpose for a commitment between two people is a legal contract and not a marriage. So-called gay marriage is not a marriage. It is a contract or commitment between two persons. It cannot be a marriage since the purpose of marriage is the production of children.

For those who have a truly distorted sex drive, one should pray for them and recognize that they also want to be loved. The so-called gay marriage can be a commitment of love, but it is not a marriage.

LOVE

Being in love is a wonderful state. The lover sees the person being loved as the most wonderful person in the world or at least the only person ever met that is so desirable. The person loved is without faults and, even if there is a fault, it is unimportant and you want to be in the presence of the loved person. I suspect being in love is a foretaste of the love of God in heaven, because God is that perfect person. I believe many of the saints experienced it. I also expect that anyone can experience that love of God on Earth if they can truly accept God on Earth.

However, coming back to earth, the state of being in love, unfortunately, fades with time and becomes love in which one another's failings become apparent.

Marrying because one is in love is a dangerous thing. Marrying is for life and, being fallible humans, it should be undertaken with serious consideration. I agree that no one is perfect and the couple marrying are not perfect. Being in love, to some extent, is self-hypnosis and therefore not reasonable. A decision to marry should be a reasonable one, not a hypnotic one.

When I think back to my own experience with love, I recognized that being in love had a lot to do with self-hypnotism. The first girl I fell in love with was Mary Anderson. I met her at the Social Forum before I started university. She was a beauty and a very nice person. The first time I saw her, she was at a meeting, and I decided then and there that she was the girl I wanted. We became girlfriend and boyfriend, and I enjoyed being with her.

Then I started university. I was very busy and saw her mainly at Social Forum meetings, where I became aware of several other girls. Two were obviously interested in me (Audrey and Elinor), but Mary was my girlfriend (although at that time I was too busy to do anything about it). I became aware that other girls were also as desirable as Mary and that my hasty decision when we first met was not necessarily a wise one. Mary was the only daughter of a well-to-do family; an outgoing person, very noticeable and a very nice person.

After ten days of visiting Elinor in the hospital, I discovered Elinor was a quiet, loving person. She had lost her father in the twenties' flu epidemic and was accustomed to hardship. Elinor accepted her injuries and months on crutches without complaint. Somehow I expected that my life would have some hard living and I wanted a wife who could accept it. I thought that Mary might find my way of life difficult. Elinor really appealed to me. I did fall in love with Elinor and spent the rest of my life loving her, but I had made a reasoned decision. I am sure that Mary and Audrey, who were obviously in love with me, would have made good wives, but it is not allowed to marry three wives. I can and do pray for them and hope I will meet them in heaven.

Working Mothers

Mothers used to be busy looking after the home and children. Today, housework requires much less time, so mothers have less to do and, as a result, leave the home for outside work. As a consequence, mothers leave their children to someone else to bring up and miss the joy of aiding their children to develop into loving, responsible, trustworthy, holy, and knowledgeable adults. In earlier times, only the very rich passed their children off to hired help, a practice that was blamed for many rich children being spoiled. Now, almost every mother passes her child off to a babysitter to raise.

Working mothers also reduce the availability of jobs for fathers. Current employment laws allow a new mother to take up to a year off to look after a newborn child and still retain their job. While a year is better than no time after a birth, a child needs much more than a year of motherly care. The major learning period of a child occurs in the early years. The basics of morals and religion are acquired at a very young age.

The modern practice of both parents working outside the home seriously limits the opportunity of children learning from their parents. Up to ten hours of the child's waking hours are spent going to, being at, and returning from the babysitter's, leaving a couple of hours for the child to learn the parents' way of life. Children are farmed out at an early age to babysitters who have a dozen or more children to look after and are interested in the child's physical, not spiritual development. Even if the babysitter is interested, she probably won't have the same points of view as the parents. In fact, if government-funded, they are probably instructed not to mention morals or religion. Plus, if they did talk religion, some of the other parents would complain.

The parents have two days a week, plus a few hours on weekdays. If the parents work hard at bringing up their children, they can probably do a sufficient job, but it does need a lot of their time.

The child's chance of acquiring the principles the parents live by is limited by available time. The parents, and the mother especially, have little of the child's awake time to instruct and guide the child. Most of the mother's available time occurs after the child has gone to bed. The reduced burden of housework due to modern equipment is an opportunity for mothers to spend more time with their children, not less. The reason for the mother of a two-parent household to work is to fill idle time and to have a wealthier lifestyle. This is unfortunate, as the extra time could be used to develop the child's character and attitude to life, to encourage and develop skills like music, and various art forms, along with an interest in gaining knowledge. All of this helps to make a better adult.

For apparent material gain, parents neglect the spiritual and cultural development of a child. The parents jeopardize the return on the most valuable investment any parent can make, the investment in a well-brought-up, loving family that they can enjoy, especially in their old age. No job outside the family can match the return on investment that raising a good family earns. One often sees childless old couples leading a worthless, lonely old age.

What is needed is work-at-home jobs for mothers, or a tax system that would make it economically worthwhile for mothers to stay at home. This would allow the mother to stay with her children, guide them, and earn an income while filling in extra time. There is pressure to introduce universal child care. Instead, why not give the cost of universal child care to mothers to stay home. Universal child care is the wrong way to go. It takes the responsibility of child-raising out of the hands of the parents and puts it into the government's hands. The communists do this to raise children to be good communists. What is your government going to raise?

CHILDREN AND CHALLENGE

Musing on children today, they appear to lead too sheltered a life. They are bused to and from school or driven by parents. They never walk because two or three blocks is too far to walk. Someone may attack them, or some other catastrophe will happen. How will they learn to look after themselves and learn independence?

When I was six-and-a-half years old, I did what children of my day did—go to school on my own. I had a 10-minute walk to the radial car stop, took the radial car to the end of the line, and then took a streetcar to the stop at the school. I enjoyed the challenge. I was not the only child doing this. I did not get kidnapped, beat up, or run over. I did learn to look after myself and learned independence.

My parents allowed me to do this. I am sure they prayed for me and my safety. They trusted me, my guardian angel, and God to keep me safe. This trust of your children and, especially, the trust in God is missing nowadays.

My children walked to and from school twice a day, about two miles. My sons went to a private high school many miles from home. I drove them to school since I was going to work and there was no suitable route by public transport. They returned home by a combination of busing, walking, and sometimes hitchhiking (although I did not approve of hitchhiking).

I benefited by the challenge of poor sight, although one does not need a physical disability to make life challenging and thus interesting. Getting to school and attending school can be presented as a challenge. Elinor and I (as well as my parents), always treated school as a challenge by encouraging our children and rewarding them on doing well, so they could realize the benefit of accepting and overcoming a challenge. Young people need challenges.

Games do present challenges, but games do not accomplish anything except winning the game, which has little, if any, real value. The real value of the game is not the winning, it is the extras you attain, such as physical exercise, experience in cooperation, and other benefits. These are the real values of sports.

Not being a sports enthusiast because of my eyesight, I encouraged my children to become active in other pursuits, such as learning to make things, camping, boating, and travelling. They were constantly encouraged to do things that produced a desirable result.

People need activities that produce something of value. Computer games do not develop physical ability. They may, to a limited extent, increase mental ability, but otherwise produce nothing of value. Once the computer game is easily solved, it becomes disinteresting because nothing of value results from playing it. Youth need to do things that have observable value. You do not find many youth playing bridge (a mentally challenging game) because it produces nothing of value. It is entertaining but not valuable.

Life without challenges is dull. Parents must strive to give their children challenges. When I wanted skis, my father gave me the tools, instructions, and materials to make my own skis. It was a real challenge, but it taught me skills, self-confidence, the satisfaction of doing a good job, and pride in my work. My skis were at least as good as, if not better than, any skis I could have bought.

Parents who try to protect their children from challenges that they can physically or mentally handle are depriving their children of opportunities to face life and conquer it. Parents who try to avoid challenges can expect their children to do likewise. It is impossible in this world to avoid challenge, and without challenges, it would be a dull world. Even adults find life dull without challenges.

An example was a young fellow who worked with me in my first job as a shipper. His father became an invalid due to an accident and could not work. They lived in the slums. One night after work, I drove him home. It was a dreary neighbourhood, but his house was brightly painted with a tidy front lawn and flowers. The other houses had muddy lawns and paint that had passed its usefulness years ago. There was such an amazing difference that I complimented him. He said, "My family make the best of whatever our situation is." Obviously, the other families did not see and accept their challenges.

The problem of youth suicide is boredom and hopelessness due to a lack of challenge. Without challenge, there are only routine activities, which are never inspiring and rarely accomplish anything of value. So a life without challenge is doing nothing and is worthless, so why live? The problem lies in not being taught to accept and overcome challenges.

How many people say a small prayer when they say goodbye to their children as they leave for school? How many people say a prayer at the start of the day or ask for God's help in their work or participating in any activity? If they did, God would give them the challenges they need to make life worth living. Those who do are not stressed or fearful people. Unfortunately, too many people never think of God; they depend entirely on themselves. They do not need God and have forgotten God.

CHILD LABOUR

Many people pick up on a cause that may be worthwhile, but never think it through. The case of child labour is one. Certainly, abusive child labour is wrong. But there is no reason why a child cannot do tasks that he or she is physically and mentally capable of doing. The children living on farms certainly help in the chores. They not only enjoy being useful, but also learn skills and attitudes that they benefit from for life. I worked for my father when I was a teenager and am very glad I did. Working for my father was invigorating and enlightening. It taught me skills I would never have acquired. One of the reasons I wanted my own business was the ability to let my children learn from work.

Child labour in underdeveloped areas, where preteens are being employed, is primarily for tasks that are of low skill. In the developed regions, machinery is doing these tasks. Undeveloped areas do not have the machinery, so to be competitive, they use child labour. In many cases, the only jobs available are low skill. Remember, the family of the labouring child may be dependent on the child, who is the only one who has a job.

The fact that as a teenager living on a small farm, I did a lot of the planting, cultivating, and harvesting, made me a useful and successful adult. It could be called child labour and today someone would have reported it, and I would have to stop.

My sons went to a private high school. Their expenses were paid for out of their earnings, from paper routes to a machining activity done at home needed by my business. Today, some activists would no doubt have complained that I was abusing my sons by allowing them to work, using child labour. It gave them experience, responsibility, and an income. Our children are exceptionally successful adults.

Organized Sports and Leisure

When I was a kid, we played hockey on a homemade rink or local pond. If you were lucky, you played on an outdoor rink in a park. Nobody had pads or special hockey skates. There were teams and scheduled games, but only the very good players played there. As a teenager during the Depression, no one had money for costly sports. We did play sports, but not in an organized fashion with schedules and referees. They were games we enjoyed, where we had fun and experienced group activities, coordination, and exercise.

When I look at the training, the schedules, and the equipment of today's sports, they appear more like work. I think the opportunities for playing sports for fun are limited today because of the general fear of everything. In supervised and controlled environments, the chances of injury or other catastrophe are limited and, therefore, parents want their children in organized sports for safety reasons. Perhaps this is good from the point of view of the child learning how to work, but it is not play. In fact, I wonder if children know how to play. They are either working at becoming expert in one or more sports or in solving a computer game. They do not play.

I enjoyed playing hockey, baseball, and rugby, but never became an expert nor did I want to. I played to play, and when I had time to play, not on a regular schedule. Sports were a low priority and never interfered with any other activities. Today, to get the advantages of exercise and coordination that sports provide, one has to be a semi-professional. It certainly takes the fun out of everyday sports.

I played on an inter-school team at St. Michael's as a lineman; we had a few practices after classes to learn how to tackle without getting hurt. The only equipment was helmets and sweaters, and the school provided them. Leisure activities for the young nowadays appear to be semi-professional sports or computer games and TV.

Growing up, reading was an important leisure activity, which aroused one's imagination and increased knowledge. My parents bought a ten-volume set of science books wherein I read every word. We also made time for artistic endeavours, such as music. I learned to play the violin. I found playing the violin (usually in the basement, to let the family sleep) relaxing after a hard day and night of studying for university. As an adult, I was good enough to play in the Arvida Symphony Orchestra. Model making, even sewing and rug hooking, were leisure time activities. We enjoyed listening to the radio (my parents chose the programs). We also had a gramophone. Again, selections were chosen by our parents and included classical music. My mother often sang along with the recordings. We did not have TV, computers, or computer games and, in some respects, I think we were better off without them.

JOHN E. BURGENER

To help mitigate the effects of the Depression on our family's lifestyle, my parents decided to buy a small farm; a couple of acres with fruit trees so we could eat no matter how severe the Depression. As a result, I grew up in a semi-farming environment. I believe this was a great advantage. Even if I had wanted to play an organized sport, we could not afford it. And my parents, who were busy improving our living accommodation, sewing clothes for the family, or preserving food, did not have the time to attend games. Instead of learning how to play hockey or another sport, I learned to build, cook, and sew.

My father, fortunately, retained his job, although with a very reduced income throughout the Depression. So, being a teenager and as the oldest in the family, the farming, was to a great extent, done by me. During spring, summer, and fall, I learned how to tend a garden, spray trees, and harvest and preserve our produce. My mother, with some help from her children, would preserve 500 quarts of fruit, vegetables, and chicken meat each year. Apples were stored in bins in the cold cellar and turned every week. Root vegetables, like carrots and turnips, were stored in barrels of sand and kept in the dark. Berries and cherries were made into jams and desserts. In the fall, before it got too cold, we would have a local farmer plough our small farm. Then, my father, my brother, and I would break up the furrows using hoes, getting the ground ready for spring planting.

I also looked after the chickens: feeding them, collecting eggs, cleaning out the chickens' stable and, the part

I did not like, killing them when they were to become food. First, I had to chase the chicken around until I caught it, then hold it with its eye looking at me while my mother chopped off its head. I improved the procedure by shooting the chicken and then chopping off its head.

There were other projects, like excavating under the house by hand to expand the cellar. In warm weather, we added two more rooms to our house. Of course, any repairs to our car were done by my dad and me.

As a spare time activity, I rebuilt an old Model T Ford truck that I salvaged from a farmer's field. By 15 years of age, I had my own hot rod, which I drove around the farmer's roads and along Indian Road where we lived. The Depression was of great benefit to me. I did things and learned skills I would never have had the opportunity to acquire in the city.

I feel sorry for those generations that followed me. Now, the greatest effort is put into learning how to play some sport and little or nothing in how to live. Everybody should know how to cook, repair clothes, and have some knowledge of mechanical and electrical workings. When I went to university, I was amazed at how few students had any concept of mechanical devices. Later, when I hired graduate physicists, some of them thought a gear train ran on tracks (it's an assembly of gears used to transfer energy).

AUTOMOBILES

When I muse on the automobile, it has gone from a great convenience to almost a necessity today. Life is very limited without it. Henry Ford made automobiles available to the general public less than a decade before my birth. I have had an automobile in my life from infancy until my 93rd birthday, when I decided my vision had reached the point where I should stop driving. My 1998 Oldsmobile is now driven by my daughter-in-law Suzanne. Although now 17 years old, it is still in use. Cars are much more durable than they were in the 1920s.

When I was about six years old, I recall my father coming home driving a new Chevrolet, called a Baby Grand. I do not know why it was called a Baby Grand because it was no smaller than others. It was a black touring car (today it would be called a convertible). It had plastic side curtains, not glass windows. The next family car I recall was a Buick sedan with glass side windows, which made it a lot more comfortable in bad weather. And, finally, the family owned a car big enough so that, when we went for a drive, my sister did not have to sit on my knee. It was a seven-passenger Cadillac (the only car that would fit our family of five children). It was a great car.

Shortly after Dad took ownership of the car, he decided to "try it out." We took a drive on the Kingston

Highway (now called Highway 2). He was driving well over the speed limit when a motorcycle got on his tail. (The police used motorcycles in those days.) Dad said, "Let's see if he can catch me." We soon lost him. I don't know how fast we were going, but I expect it was over ninety miles an hour. My father was very pleased with the car's performance.

The top cars in the 1920s had the performance of the average car today. They lacked many of the features though, such as air conditioning, radios, heated seats, or automatic seat adjustment.

In my late teens, Dad bought a LaSalle (a smaller version of the Cadillac). It was quite a flashy car with a spare tire on each side at the front. He traded it for a Dodge during the war because it was too hard on gas (gas being rationed) and needed tires (also not readily available).

When we moved to Lorne Park, I noticed an abandoned truck in a neighbouring farmer's field. I asked the farmer if I could have it if I arranged to have it towed out. He was glad to get rid of it. My father agreed to drive in and tow the truck out. By spring, I had succeeded in getting it running first by stripping it down to the front end and then scavenging parts from the wreckers and dumps. At 15 years old, I had a working hot rod.

My friend Roy Fraser, who lived on Indian Road, had a Chevrolet truck that had burned. I traded him my working Model T Ford for his burned-out Chevy. I soon had the Chevy stripped down and running. It was much faster and more powerful than the Ford. Now we both had hot rods.

At 16, I took ownership of a 1927 Chevrolet and converted the hot rod into a tractor by replacing the rear wheel assembly with a truck assembly and putting a second transmission in the drive train. In low gear, with both transmissions, it had terrific power. My father used it on his small farm until he retired to Florida.

My hot rods and tractor taught me a great deal about cars and mechanical devices. It also gave me self-confidence, which I am sure helped me to accomplish many of the things I did in my life.

Automobiles in my youth were much simpler and not as durable. I remember a winter trip to my grandfather's factory. Some changes were needed in the factory, and my father and my Uncle Chris were going to help out. It started snowing as we left. By the time we reached the big hill on the Dundas Highway, the snow was quite deep. The car was having trouble getting up the hill, so Uncle Chris and I got out to push. We made some headway but obviously we were not going to make it up the hill. Dad pulled off the road and had to jack up the back wheels and put tire chains on. With the chains, we made it to the top of the hill. Now we had to remove the chains because driving any distance would wear them out. We had to go through this process again on a hill near the factory. The side curtains did not keep the snow out, so the inside of the car was loaded with snow. A trip of a hundred miles in the winter was a major undertaking; you took blankets, tire chains, a jack, and a tow rope.

The car that was bought to drive my siblings and me to school was a 1927 Ford Model T. Unfortunately, it could not take the daily grind of 50 miles and was constantly giving trouble. So my father bought me a 1927 Chevrolet. It performed well and continued to get us to school for the rest of that school year. My continued ownership of the Chevrolet was conditional on me maintaining it in good working order and paying for my own operating expenses.

The Chevy required an overhaul each fall and had a problem with the rear axle breaking without warning. I had learned a lot about cars with my hot rods. I kept my car in good working order, from first-year high school to third-year university.

After I had it for a couple of years, I loaned it to the Danforth Technical School where my uncle, Jim Hogarth, was a teacher of motor mechanics, to train students for two months. They re-bored the cylinders and replaced cast iron pistons with over-sized aluminum pistons, changed the carburetor for a later version, and beefed up the suspension. It greatly improved performance. The top speed before the improvements was 55 mph. After the changes, the car reached 85 mph, but it consumed more fuel and gasoline had risen to 30 cents a gallon.

A police check on older cars (it was 13 years old) found that the emergency brake was not up to par, and I was given one week to repair or scrap the car. I was too busy at university to do anything about it and could not afford the repair, so I sold it for $50 to a wrecker. It was a good car and served me for eight years.

Cars, in general, lasted five years if heavily used. In northern areas, where salt was used on the roads, the car bodies would rust out in two to three years, so you had to have body repair or buy a new car. In my business, employees who had company cars received a new car every five years or 100,000 miles. In my busiest years, I averaged about 100,000 miles in a little over two years, and the car would still be useful, but I did not want a breakdown on a business trip.

I did some heavy driving. I would drive to Montreal, leaving home at 5:00 a.m., to do a day's business and drive home the same night, getting home a little after midnight. I often drove to and from Ottawa on the same day. The speed limits were higher back then, and I admit that they did not mean much to me. I always watched for police, and with the help of a citizen band radio, I knew where the areas were to slow down. Only once was I charged with speeding—on a return trip to Montreal.

It was a couple of days before Christmas, and I had left Montreal late. When I crossed into Ontario, where the speed limit was 70 mph, I sped up to 100 mph. (I always maintain that if you are not alert enough to see the traffic cop, you should not be speeding.) Around Kingston, I saw lights pacing me, so I ducked in front of the truck and slowed to 80 mph. I thought I should let the traffic cop get something. Shortly, there was a police car behind me, and the officer signalled to pull over. He gave me a ticket for ten miles above the speed limit that carried no consequences.

Then he said, "All right, you have a ticket for 80 miles an hour, and I know you could have slowed down to seventy. How fast were you going? I followed you for 20 miles at speeds over 100 miles an hour and could not gain on you."

He also said, "I recognize that you were alert enough to spot me and slow down, so how fast were you going?"

"You caught me. I was going 80."

"Come on! How fast were you going?"

"Eighty miles an hour!"

"You liar!" he said. "Get going."

I held the speed down to the limit the rest of the way because, although friendly, he probably radioed ahead to watch for me.

On a trip from Ottawa along Highway 7, I was driving well above the speed limit and passed a car parked at the side of the road with a man standing in front of it. As I looked back in the rear-view mirror, he got into his car but did not drive away. It struck me that he was a spotter, so I slowed to ten miles below the limit.

A few miles later, a policeman flagged me down. He said I was speeding. I objected and asked how he measured my speed. He was standing on the road. He said I had passed a speed check farther back.

This was before electronic speed checks were available. The rule was a police car had to follow you for a quarter mile, or time you over a measured distance to charge you. I pointed this out and also mentioned that he could not claim he had timed me because I spotted the spotter and drove below the limit over the distance timed and would fight any charges in court. He did not give me a ticket.

The fastest I have ever driven was in Nevada, where there are no speed limits. I drove my Oldsmobile Toronado at 145 mph, and it still had acceleration. On another occasion, I was late starting on a trip to a conference in Edmonton. I drove to the Lake of the Woods area the first day. On the second day, after I passed Winnipeg, I took the north road. On this highway, there were hardly any villages and almost no traffic.

On several occasions, I drove to Chicago in the morning and back at night. The speed limit on the interstate roads was 80 mph in those days. A 500-mile drive was less than six hours. On another occasion, I drove from Salt Lake City to Mississauga in two days.

I preferred driving to planes because, in many cases, it actually took less travel time, and I had a car at my disposal and was free to go home when ready. Adding up all the time of going to the airport, the flight time, and getting a car rental and return, driving was often as quick. I will admit that traffic has increased substantially in recent years and the speeds at which I drove are not possible today.

I have driven on European roads where traffic was heavy and at speeds over 100 mph and felt safe. I think the European highway drivers are probably more experienced. The cautionary slow down areas on the German Autobahn are 80 mph. I have driven on Italian roads at 200 km/h and had a Maserati come up behind me with its lights flashing and pass me going at least 250 km/h.

SMOKING

Smoking was a form of relaxation for most people. People feeling stress often took a break and had a smoke. Afterwards, they were refreshed and able to get back to whatever was happening.

While a lot of effort has been put into showing the damage excessive smoking can cause, there have been no studies on how effective cessation from smoking has actually been in reducing cancer or any other effect. Before smoking was declared evil and almost criminal, most people who were inclined to be stressed would relax by smoking. Cancer happened, but not very commonly. Today, with almost no one in Canada smoking, almost every family I know has someone suffering from cancer or has died from it. My son's wife, Paula, died of colon cancer in 2008. She was one of many whom John knew who had died in the past six years from colon cancer. My son, Peter, died of brain cancer in 2014. My son Paul had prostate cancer in 2016. Several of my nieces and nephew's children have had cancer. Many of my friends have died from cancer. In my experience, cancer has increased unbelievably in direct proportion to the number of people who have stopped smoking. The less we smoke, the more kinds of cancer and more people seem to get cancer.

There needs to be some thinking and possibly less scientific research about cancer. Cancer of every kind occurs in otherwise healthy people. There does not seem to be any specific cause of cancer. It appears to happen in all kinds of circumstances and lifestyles, irrespective of the person's health. Although specific causes are given, they usually refer to theory. The widespread occurrence appears to indicate that an underlying and not an apparent basic cause is the real problem. All those whom I have known to contract cancer were uptight people. They tended to lead stressful lives.

In our modern society, we are constantly warned of all the serious catastrophes that are happening or will happen (terrorism, nuclear energy, climate change, environmental catastrophes), along with a host of other things to worry about. Those who are worriers are constantly stressed and, I believe, are candidates for contracting cancer. The cancers are of the stomach, brain, and colon and are all affected by stress. The common denominator is stress. In the 1930s, there were cancers and one knew of a few cases, but today everyone knows someone or has a relative who is suffering from cancer.

In the 1930s, we did not have environmentalists and the United Nations to constantly warn us of all the serious things that were going to happen, so people were not as stressed. Also, people were smoking. Smoking reduced stress enough to *prevent* most cancers. I would love to see a study done to check on the real benefits of not smoking. Possibly the legalization of marijuana will replace smoking as a stress reliever. Tobacco did not affect one's brain or cause hallucinations. I believe that tobacco is a better stress reliever than marijuana, but the fanatical anti-tobacco lobby will no doubt disagree.

DRUGS & ALCOHOL

Drugs have their legitimate use. Morphine is called God's own medicine. When properly used, it is a gift from God. Abused, it is a terrible curse.

Even over-indulging in simple foods can cause problems, such as obesity or the reverse problem of anorexia. We do not attack the problem of obesity by banning the use of food. I suspect that if we were to ban certain fat-producing foods, there would be an increase in consumption. The people who want to ban certain foods in schools cannot stop the students from eating them. It would probably increase their consumption because students who never ate them will consider it smart to consume them.

The prohibition of alcohol taught Canadians to drink. Drunkenness was widespread during Prohibition. Since alcohol was illegal, it was smart to drink. There were bootleggers out there who would convince you that drinking alcohol was smart and fun.

As a boy, I recall seeing more drunkenness than is seen today. For example, on a trip from Toronto to Kingston (about 180 miles), we had taken a back road to avoid traffic and came upon two buses parked at the side of the road. Thinking they had a problem, we stopped. Everyone in the buses was drunk except the pushers and the drivers. Bootlegging was common, as experienced on a visit to my mother's parents, who had a farm in Pennsylvania. While we were there, two different bootleggers knocked on my grandparents' door, offering alcohol.

The licensing of alcohol instead of suppression, while not eliminating drunkenness, has made it less prevalent today than during Prohibition. Licensing has provided a source of government revenue instead of an expense. It has also eliminated the bootleggers. No one is getting rich by encouraging individuals to drink alcohol except perhaps the alcohol producers, who are controlled.

Since street drugs, by law, are forbidden for general use, the user must use these clandestinely. This has three harmful effects: the user cannot be supervised and assisted; it becomes attractive and seen as smart or daring (many will try it because it is forbidden); and the pushers can make money by selling it. The pushers work hard to encourage more people to take drugs. On the other hand, if such drugs were available in a drug store, the monetary incentives for the drug dealers would decline, thus reducing their numbers. It would no longer be considered smart or daring to take drugs. Also, if one did become addicted, no law would be broken, and the person could get help.

In the 1920s, you could buy any drug at the local drug store. There were no pushers, no drug dealers and, without a doubt, fewer addicts. Many of the addicts received treatment. I think the present system is insane.

We do not suppress car use because some people drive too fast or are not good drivers; we penalize those who do not follow the rules. A sensible means of controlling drug use is to penalize the excessive use of drugs.

We should legalize the use of drugs and make the drugs available in drug stores with suitable restrictions, as they were in the 1920s. Excessive use of drugs would result in punishment or loss of medical benefits. Then the prospective user would face punishment or the misery of drug addiction without help. Certainly, there might be a few sad cases, but there would be no drug dealers, and prospective users would seriously consider its use. Added to these advantages, the government would save billions of dollars now used to combat drug dealing.

Drug control really plays out as a fight between the drug cartels and government drug control groups in which the addict is a victim. Billions are earned by the cartels because of the billions spent by the drug enforcement agencies. The fight appears to be won by the cartels. It could all be stopped by legalizing drug use as we do for alcohol. The cartels would disappear, the addicts could be treated using the savings, and the government would receive the revenue.

I might also ask, what gives us the right to try to prevent people from making a free-will decision that only affects them and not others when we try to prevent them from taking drugs? Surely there must be some in our government who can see the hopelessness of drug suppression. They did wake up to alcohol.

Appetites

We probably never stop to think about our appetites, but they play an important role in our lives. Free will makes us personally responsible for all our actions. It also allows us to do things that do not conform to our true nature. Animals, having no free will, do not have responsibility for their actions, nor do they have to be concerned about actions that do not conform to their nature. They act according to their instincts. Humans, on the other hand, have free will and what they do is a personal choice, not controlled by instinct or anything else. Some actions may be restricted by law for the common good, but other than that a human can do anything they are physically or mentally capable of doing. This includes satisfying our appetites.

The appetites make necessary activities pleasant so that we can enjoy doing them. The human has complete control and is personally responsible for their use of the appetites. Uncontrolled appetites usually become routine and result in addiction, such as drugs or alcohol, gluttony or anorexia. Drugs and alcohol have their legitimate uses, when used in a reasonable manner, and are a great boon to humanity.

Sex is an appetite no different than any appetite. It is an important one and, like all appetites, can be abused. Its primary purpose is the continuation of the race. Since it is important to continue the race, it is a very pleasurable experience.

A human offspring takes many years of development to become an independent person. Because of this lengthy period, it is widely accepted that sex should be restricted to a single couple. It is also necessary to restrict the sex appetite so that the parents have sufficient time to engage in the child's development. Indiscriminate sex is not conducive to the proper development of families and thus society.

Any form of uncontrolled sex is a distortion of the sexual appetite, like overeating is a distortion of a necessary activity. Homosexuality cannot produce offspring, which is the purpose of the sex appetite. I find it difficult to see any difference between homosexuality and alcoholism, or any addiction. Sex is an appetite that must be controlled. Otherwise, why punish rape or condemn promiscuity?

The destruction of Sodom and Gomorrah in Genesis 19 was the result of the sin of sodomy. Angels appeared to Abraham and told him their mission. Abraham petitioned God to agree that if only ten men were not homosexual, God would save the city. It was finalized when Lot protected the angels from being raped by the men of Sodom. God does not approve of sodomy.[1]

In some cases, there does seem to be a malfunction of the sex appetite, and some are born with a compromised sexual appetite. Humans are born with afflictions of many kinds and are to be loved and assisted. A truly distorted sexual appetite is certainly an affliction that is difficult to endure. I am not capable of judging their activities, but I believe that a person suffering from such an affliction will receive graces to compensate and gain great merit if they control their distorted appetite. For those who commit sodomy without an affliction, it is the sin of sodomy.

I believe the gay parades were started as a way to move society to accept gay people; however, they have degenerated into a celebration of the sin of sodomy. Homosexual activity is definitely an unnatural activity and, as such, is a sin. Those who turn out for the parade and those participating are celebrating the sin. It is hard to believe that God is pleased by such a parade. We should not celebrate the sin, but should pray for them and show our love. The world is in a mess because we are running it without God's help.

---

1 Editor's note: The destruction of Sodom and Gomorrah is considered by Biblical experts today as a punishment for evilness that related to many factors, especially lack of respect for strangers which was essential in that era. Abraham argued for sparing the cities if ten righteous men were found, not if non-homosexual men were found. Dad's interpretation is based on the older teachings of many churches, but is no longer considered a valid historically correct interpretation of the event.

Control of One's Life

Abortion, euthanasia, and contraception are claimed to be means of controlling one's life. The Catholic Church teaches that these actions are wrong. They have only become right in the general view since technology made them right. For at least four thousand years (since the beginning of the Hebrew story), society has deemed these actions to be wrong. No one has come up with a good moral argument that they are right.

Abortion, euthanasia, and contraception are bad for the state. Canada is losing its Canadian population because Canadians do not have a replacement level of children due to abortion and birth control. The population is rapidly becoming new immigrants, not Canadians. All arguments in favour of birth control, abortion, and euthanasia are based on convenience, not moral arguments.

There is little in life we actually control. You can make choices, but you control almost nothing. You cannot control your birth, your parents, or your siblings, and the person you married was probably a chance encounter. There are few controls over the people you will meet in your lifetime. Your job is controlled by your boss or your customers. No one has control over the illnesses or accidents you have. Where you live is a choice, although you still live according to the society around you. Control of your life is a myth.

The sixth commandment given by God to Moses was "Thou shalt not kill." Euthanasia is killing and, therefore, forbidden by God. If you have no belief or interest in God, then killing is only a concern of the law. Christ suffered on the cross, demonstrating that life was not a bowl of cherries. The reason you are dying of an incurable sickness could be that you are being given the opportunity to perform Christ's work on Earth. For example, I know of a woman with an incurable disease who, instead of killing herself, is spending her time helping others with similar diseases to cope. This is a more human way of facing a difficulty, and I am sure more pleasing to God.

Similarly, abortion is killing. The sixth commandment does not specify what is not to be killed; it just states killing is wrong. Abortion is killing a life. One may argue that an embryo is not yet a human. Even so, it must have a human soul, or it would not become a human. It is a living being, destined to live with God and, therefore, is valuable in God's eyes. As Jesus said, the Father knows when a sparrow falls (Matt 10:29). If God is concerned about a sparrow, He is certainly concerned about humans. Miscarriage is a common happening, usually not due to any fault of the woman; obviously, such cases are not voluntary abortion. In some cases, and possibly in most cases, the miscarriage is due to some irregularity in the pregnancy and is thus a blessing for the parents that a deformed child is not born. Abortion, probably because of inconvenience, destroys a beautiful human, capable of human life and knowing God and is, therefore, is a condemnable act.[2]

Conception is a natural and necessary function that occurs as a result of a free will. The only living beings capable of preventing conception are humans. Because of the God-given gift of free will, humans can frustrate the natural effects of their actions and prevent conception.

Contraception is a free will choice and therefore a responsible choice. It is neutral—neither good nor evil—depending on the reason for the choice. I find it hard to see it as neutral or good, since one is frustrating a natural process for the purpose of pleasure or for some other purpose. The culpability of the other purpose would have to involve God. The determination of the size of a family must be defined by God and the person. If God

---

2 Editor's note: While I agree that abortion is killing, and the child is human from conception, however, there are times when killing is generally considered as appropriate, such as in wars. What I feel that Dad has missed is that the soul grows as the body grows. There is merit in living a long life as it allows the soul to grow to maturity. A just starting-to-grow human soul is not a fully developed or immortal soul any more than a stem cell in a drop of blood has an immortal soul. Stem cells are the ones that can grow into other cell types and in theory can be used to clone a person. When you have a cut that bleeds, one does not worry about the potential loss of the stem cells. An embryo's soul is much less developed than the soul of a dog or cat until long after conception. I do not personally have a problem with abortion any more than I have a problem with killing cows or chickens for meat. This is still much debated in the world. Dad follows the Catholic Church teachings in most topics, and his views are what this book is about. But in some cases, I disagree enough that I feel it important to say so.

is not involved in the decision, it is not a valid decision, since all life is due to God. How can too large a family be a justifiable reason for contraception when an act of self-control, as reasonable people are expected to use, could have the same effect?

When Elinor and I married, we decided that we did not want to have a child for at least a year. We quickly discovered that Elinor's menstrual cycle was too erratic to use the rhythm method, so we abstained from sex for the first year and probably loved one another more because of it. It can be done.

OVERPOPULATION

The United Nations and other short-sighted organizations claim the world is overpopulated. I have done some musing on this using data provided by Google. Let's look at some of it.

Google lists the population densities in 241 locations; 199 out of 241 locations have less than 100 people per square kilometer.

Table 1: The ten most populous areas of the world

Location	# people per km2
Macau	18,534
Monaco	16,933
Singapore	7,714
Gibraltar	4,659
Vatican City	1,877
Malta	1,322
Bermuda	1,226
St. Martin	1,101
Maldives	1,037

Table 2: Comparison of countries' populations per km2 and number of countries with that population range.

Population per km2	Number of Countries
More than 1,000	10
500 to 1,000	21
300 to 500	47
200 to 300	63
100 to 200	110
50 to 100	150
less than 50	91 out of 241
World average	50.3

World Population = 7.5×10^9 or 7,500,000,000 people
Land area = 29% of 510×10^6 km^2 = 149×10^6 km^2
Average # of people per km^2 = $7500 \times 10^6 \div 149 \times 10^6$ = 50.3 people per km^2

That is 91 out of 241 countries with densities of less than the average. The world could easily handle 14 billion people and, using the average noted above, would represent a density of only 100 persons per km^2. Projecting that would mean an increase of about 0.9% in the Maldives' population density and a 2% increase in Gibraltar's (which I did not find overcrowded when I visited there).

Of course, the UN and the prophets of doom are screaming about overpopulation, just as they did when I was a teenager in the 1930s. They also claimed that if we ever had another war, all the coal reserves would be used up, the world would run out of energy, and we would be living in the dark, freezing. All the leading newspapers propagated this.

Looking at the table from Google, if world population doubled, only 150 out of 241 countries would have a population density of over 100—still quite low.

Table 3: Populations, per km2, of selected countries

Country	Persons per km2
Canada	3.4
Argentina	14
Brazil	24
USA	34
Kenya	114
Nigeria	114
Germany	229
Great Britain	255
Japan	349
Belgium	355

To bring the average population up to the level of Great Britain (the people of Great Britain do not consider themselves overpopulated) would require a world population of over 38 billion. A world population at that level would certainly require some changes, but humans surely have the intelligence to handle it. I do not think we have to worry about overpopulation. We just have to be more Christ-like and love our neighbour.

The problem in Africa is not overpopulation, but corrupt governments and tribalism, neither of which is loving your neighbour. Most of the world is willing to help, as long as it is not in their backyard. Here, the great fear of inadequacy rears its head. The world is afraid of any change, and a higher population could possibly cause change. Intelligent change should be welcomed, but changes are feared in this godless world.

Japan is a country that has a high population density (349 people per km^2), with few resources. Argentina has a density of 14 and has lots of resources. Great Britain and Germany are not overcrowded; somewhere in the 250 range. Places like Macau, with a population more than 70 times that of Britain, still have a high standard of living in an area with virtually no resources. Much of Africa is living at a subsistence level, with population densities below the 100 level, yet has tremendous potential resources.

The United States has a population density of 34 and Canada has a density of less than 4. The same applies to most of South America; Brazil is 23 and Argentina is 16. A world population of 7.5 billion, as the UN claims, is only an average world density of 50 people per km^2, assuming only 30% of the world's surface is livable. It is not a problem of overpopulation. It is simply that nobody wants to be bothered with solutions, as these may make difficulties for them.

Food production is presently derived from 13% of the Earth's surface, and at least 20% of that acreage is fallow. The increasing population would use up more land surface. The Sahara Desert is almost 13% of the Earth's surface and has fertile soil. The ingenuity of man must surely be able to develop ways of using presently unusable areas such as the arctic, deserts, mountains, and even the sea.

Sea greenhouses desalinate sea water by sunlight and require no energy input. Vineyards in Europe have been established on mountainsides. With irrigation, deserts could supply the world with food. Desalination is a viable solution to sourcing water. The current processing cost is as low as a few cents a gallon and would probably diminish further with extensive use. The greatest expense is pumping, yet there seems to be no difficulty pumping oil across continents.

A possible future solution to the food supply is similar to the WWII Victory Gardens. People were encouraged to turn their backyards into vegetable gardens. Similarly, apartment dwellers were encouraged to use their decks. Parks grew vegetables instead of flowers. Why not construct gardens on flat-roofed buildings?

There are many ways living could be changed without great difficulty to accommodate huge increases in population. It is not a problem of overpopulation; rather, it is an unwillingness to find solutions. It may be impossible for shallow-minded man, but not for God.

God told Adam to increase and multiply and fill the world. It is far from full. The real problem is ignoring God's command to love your neighbour. Canada alone could take many millions of immigrants, but we do not want such people. It would be very upsetting if we were to do so. I think God's plan is to follow Macau and increase immigration and birth rates.

In my opinion, the world is far from overpopulated, and I expect we are far from God's command to fill the world. Whatever the population, there will always be shallow-minded prophets of doom with limited vision who will predict dire consequences that never happen.

Is Climate Change a World Conspiracy?

Through my musings, I have become convinced that the United Nations has persuaded the majority of current world leaders, including many scientists, of global climate change due to carbon dioxide.

The climate has been changing for 4.3 billion years—since the world began. There have been many ice ages and many warm periods, all without the help of humans. The world survived them all. If the climate were not changing, then there would be something to worry about. Man's effect on the climate is minuscule compared to the natural mechanism of climate. Has any man or group of men stopped a rainfall or changed winter into summer? The claim that carbon dioxide produced by industry is going to cause serious damage to the world's climate is not only false, but it is also an inane statement.

Billions of animals have been producing carbon dioxide with every breath for millions of years. Thousands of volcanoes in every eruption pour billions of tons of carbon dioxide into the air. Even today, hundreds of volcanoes are pouring huge amounts of carbon dioxide into the air. Decaying organic matter and forest and grass fires have been putting enormous amounts of carbon dioxide into the atmosphere for billions of years. By now, if carbon dioxide accumulated in the atmosphere, the atmosphere should be carbon dioxide, not oxygen and nitrogen.

The absolutely unfounded theory of climate change by carbon dioxide equilibrium is fantasy. There is not the slightest evidence to support such an absurd theory, yet the UN advocates it, and a huge number of thoughtless scientists, media, politicians, and environmentalists blindly follow it.

Rainfall removes carbon dioxide. Anyone who drinks Coke or a carbonated drink knows that water dissolves copious amounts of carbon dioxide. One liter of water at $5°$ C dissolves 2.27 grams of carbon dioxide (almost 2 liters of carbon dioxide). Rain is condensed water vapour. At the moment of condensation, it is ultra-pure and one of the most powerful solvents on Earth. Carbon dioxide and the so-called greenhouse gases are readily dissolved, making it impossible for these gases to accumulate in the atmosphere.

The following information can be found in any scientific handbook of physical tables, even on Google. These simple high school science calculations show the foolishness of the conspiracy.

1 cubic centimeter is 1 milliliter; therefore, 1cm of rain over 1 square cm is 1 ml of water.

1 cm of rain over 1 square meter is 100 cm x 100 cm = 10,000 milliliters of rain per square meter, or 10 liters.

1 square km is 1,000 meters x 1,000 meters = 1 million square meters.

In 1 cm or 10 mm of rain (less than a ½ inch), each square km receives 10 million liters of rain.

Water at 5°C (approximate air temperature at cloud level) dissolves 2.27g of CO_2 per liter approximately.

1 cm of rainfall over 1 square km is 10 million liters of rain, and dissolves 23 million grams (23,000 kg) of CO_2. This removes 23 metric tons of CO_2 from the atmosphere.

The area of the Earth is $510 \times 10^6 \, km^2$.

The average annual worldwide rainfall is 99 cm.

The amount of carbon dioxide removed yearly is: $510 \times 10^6 \, km^2$ x 99cm x 23 Metric tons of CO_2 per km^2 per cm of rain = $1,161,270 \times 10^6$ or $1,161 \times 10^9$ Metric tons

So, 1,161 billion metric tons of CO_2 can be removed from the atmosphere annually by rain without considering the millions of other carbon sinks—35 times the carbon dioxide produced by man. Rainfall makes it impossible for carbon dioxide to build up in the atmosphere. The carbon dioxide equilibrium theory is unfounded nonsense. [NOAA estimate 35 billion metric tons of CO_2 are produced by humans each year at present]

The greenhouse effect of carbon dioxide and other gases present in a few hundred parts per million is minuscule compared to tens of thousands of parts per million of water vapour with a much broader absorption range. The clouds are water vapour, not carbon dioxide. Climate change due to carbon dioxide is an unimaginably stupid scam.

The ignorance or dishonesty of thousands of scientists is a disgrace and leads one to question the reliability of science. It is also amazing that so many environmentalist, politicians, and media are so easily taken in by such a conspiracy, a conspiracy promoted by the United Nations, which receives billions each year to study "climate change" and wants to acquire worldwide control of industry with an army to enforce it, as the Kyoto II Accord demonstrated.

Carbon dioxide emissions are a factor of worldwide industry. The ability to convince the immense number of gullible people would give the conspirators worldwide control of industry and control of the world—something to be worried about.

GLOBAL CLIMATE CONTROL MECHANISM

For the general public and the ignorant scientists, the global climate mechanism is controlled mainly by water vapour.

High school science demonstrates that when a gram of water (a very small amount) evaporates, it takes a lot of heat (595.5 calories) out of the environment. Similarly, when a gram of moisture condenses into water, 595.5 calories are put into the environment. A kilogram of water vapour, on condensing, releases 595,500 calories. Rainfall of 1 centimeter over an area of 1 square kilometer condenses 10 million liters of water, putting 6 billion calories of heat into the air or removes 6 billion calories when evaporated. Dew occurs because the air is cooling at night and water vapour gives up its heat and becomes water, warming the night air. Water vapour—in percent levels, equivalent to tens of thousands of parts per million being generated by sunlight on the oceans, which cover 70% of the Earth's surface—controls the climate, not a few parts per million of carbon dioxide.

As the simple high school level science above shows, climatic problems with CO_2 in the atmosphere and the greenhouse effect are fantasy. Why have so many scientists, politicians, media, and environmentalists accepted this totally unscientific scam?

The widespread narrowness of thinking and the acceptance of this scam is very disturbing. It demonstrates, even in this enlightened age, how easily a conspirator can take over. Hitler, by promoting his scam of *lebensraum* (living space), convinced the German people to commit some of the world's worst crimes. Is the world about to accept a world Hitler? This global warming or climate change scam is promoted by the UN, which is an organization that could easily lead the world to commit similar crimes against humanity. The United Nations is made up of 180 nations (less than 50 are democracies, and the others are corrupt dictatorships), many of whom would no doubt be happy to get control of the world.

Climate change has cost and is costing governments and businesses billions of dollars. It has spawned international conferences, carbon credits, carbon taxes, government policies such as clean energy, and even an attempt at the Kyoto II Accord, which would have given the UN control of the world's industry and an army to enforce it. Many beneficial projects have been rejected or delayed based on the scam. Its effect on the world has been and is unbelievable. The religious would say it is the most successful endeavour of Satan since Hitler. Its scope seems to be beyond the capacity of the world. This conspiracy is based on science that a high school student could prove wrong. Its endorsement by a large portion of the scientific community is a most unimaginably disgraceful scientific failure. The reliability of science is seriously brought into question.

I believe that the fears and gullibility that burned witches are still widely prevalent in this supposedly enlightened world that has forgotten God and where witch burning is still available to the unscrupulous.

EXISTENCE

All science is studying some form of existence. A scientist should have an understanding of existence. The philosopher Aristotle and many since have struggled to understand existence. They have attempted to describe existence in terms of logic. I suggest existence should be treated in the same manner as the physical sciences.

The physical science approach is to develop a theory from observed phenomena and then test it on other observable phenomena. Concrete logical proof, in general, is not possible. For example, there is no possibility of logically proving that the sun exists. We can see its light and feel its warmth, but there is no way we can prove logically that it is the sun. It has become accepted as a fact and universally accepted as an obvious fact that needs no proof. This applies to all scientific theories.

The first thing we observe is that existence takes many forms, from the simplest inanimate object (a grain of sand) to the most complicated existence (the human brain). Although we cannot touch, see, or hear a thought, the thought has existence. We can observe the effects of immaterial existence, such as a thought or an emotion, by its effect on material objects. There are existences, such as light or radio waves, that are not solid matter but which are detected by physical means and are material. The most intriguing existence that we can observe is life. Why life came into being, we really don't know. However, once it became part of existence in the world, it blossomed.

There are different levels of existence. A rock is a piece of matter that cannot do anything different than be a rock. A tree has existence, but its level of existence is higher than a rock; the tree changes, it grows, and it seeks light, all within itself. The tree follows its nature. It cannot choose an alternate way. It does not have free will, but it does have the ability to do things on its own and to produce existences similar to itself. This ability to do things by itself and produce offspring is defined as a living existence. Therefore, a tree has a living existence higher than the level of a rock. A dog can do more things than a tree and has a higher level of living existence than a tree. A human has an even higher level of living existence and can also make intelligent choices based on information presented.

The rock has an inanimate or material existence. It consists of matter only and possesses no apparent immaterial characteristics. Material existences can be revitalized by replacing parts. The tree, the dog, and the human are living existences. Living existence embodies something other than matter. When a living existence ceases to function (dies) because of a malfunctioning component, it cannot be brought back to life by replacing a component. (Only while still alive can a malfunctioning part be replaced and life continued.) For a deceased living existence, the matter is still there, but something has gone. Unlike any other system, it immediately starts to decay. The immaterial life has gone. Life is something we cannot directly observe or measure. Let's call the living element the life force.

All living existences that we can observe consist of a material existence that we can see, feel, and measure. We can only recognize the immaterial life force due to the activities that it allows in matter. The very simplest form of life is a single cell, which can reproduce itself by splitting. Reproducing does something a non-living existence cannot do. For higher levels of life, thoughts exist but are not matter. We are familiar with thoughts, feelings, impressions, and many more non-material existences that are found in living existences.

What is a thought? There are routine thoughts, such as "I need a drink." There are creative thoughts, such as a poem or the design of a building. Animals have routine thoughts. Humans and many animals are builders and, therefore, can visualize what they intend to build. Building requires the ability to imagine. Humans can imagine and are capable of creating. Insofar as animals can imagine, they can create. Many animals and birds build and produce new existence, such as a nest or a beaver lodge, and use primitive tools. In so doing, they have thoughts and are producing existence. Living existences have the potential of being a builder at the level of their living existence and physical capability.

We cannot touch, see, or feel a thought, but it does have existence. A thought can exist in a being with a brain capable of thinking. A rock cannot have a thought. A thought is best described as an immaterial image or process that can originate in a human and in other

advanced living existences. The thought image is dependent on the thinker for its existence. A poem first exists
as an image. Unless written or spoken so that others can
see or hear it, its existence is entirely dependent on the
thinker. For a thought to exist outside the thinker in a
material world, it must be given material existence with
existing material substance. There are also dreams, visions,
inspirations, and emotions that are not material but which
have existence and occur in humans and possibly in other
living existences.

Mental telepathy is experienced by many people.
Dogs and other animals also appear to experience it. It is
also quite common for a thought or its result to appear
more or less simultaneously in many places—a thought's
existence is being shared. This may happen because the
conditions are right for it to happen.

Another aspect of life is concern for one's offspring.
As we move up the scale of living existence, the concern
for one's offspring grows. Trees and plants protect their
seeds with hard shells, drop them, and have no more
concern. Fish lay their eggs in a safe place; some travel
up rivers far from their habitat. Reptiles seem more concerned about their offspring and bury their eggs close
to water. Birds make nests and tend the eggs and the
hatched chicks. Mammals care for their offspring until
adulthood. Humans protect and love their offspring for
life and even after death. Humans even attempt to protect
their thoughts, or art, or other expressions of existence.
It appears that life not only wants to share its existence,

but also wants to protect its created or shared existences. To protect and wish good for anything is to love.

It appears that the capacity to love increases with the level of living existence. The love humans have of themselves exists. Love cannot be described in physical dimensions; it is immaterial and therefore cannot be recognized by our physical senses. However, one can experience an awareness of love, both given and received, which is not due to our senses. It would appear that humans and other living existences have an awareness that is independent of our senses.

A dog is devoted to its master (surely a form of love), but this devotion, although recognized by a dog's actions, is an awareness the dog has that cannot be explained or measured. It appears that living existences have awareness—some may call it feelings—that are dimensionless and are not sensed by our material senses. Therefore, they are not material and must be functions of the life force or mind.

The world is full of beauty. Beauty is well-ordered, as distinct from disorder, and is described as an experience of pleasure, meaning, or satisfaction. Sunset and sunrise display a canvas few, if any, artists can duplicate. The rocks, the mountains, the landscape, the flora, the animal life, and the humans are all pleasant to see. The universe, as we see it—the sun, the moon, and the stars—are well-ordered and unimaginably beautiful. There is little, if anything, in nature that is not well-ordered and beautiful.

One may argue that beauty is in the eye of the beholder. The statement should say the interpretation of beauty is in the eye of the beholder. Beauty exists whether the beholder appreciates it or not. Since all existence, in general, is beautiful, beauty must be a characteristic of existence.

Another aspect of living and non-living existence is the tendency toward complexity. Complexity is characterized as something of many parts in an intricate arrangement or interconnection. If one considers that life on Earth started as a single cell and evolved to the complexity of the human brain, the striving for complexity is strong. And it is not confined to life existences—even rocks strive for complexity. Minerals formed from molten lava, on solidifying, end up as complex crystals. Awareness, intelligence, capacity to build, beauty, and the level of the ability to love, all increase with complexity in living existence.

Human creations start as a thought. In fact, everything done by humans in this world starts as a thought. Anything human-made requires that a human pre-existed the product and was accomplished by persons expressing their intelligence and using their existence.

The most powerful aspect of living matter is claimed to be the urge to reproduce. The very essence of living existence is to produce new living existence. The higher forms of life (male and female) generate new life by sharing a mutual act. The shared existences are not duplicates of the parents but resemble the parents. All living existences are produced by living existences and start as a simple cell. As the cell develops, it goes through the complete ancestry from the first living cell, sharing the life of the first living existence—an amazing process.

Although the living existence is sharing the immaterial life of the first life, it has an independent life existence. Humans share their existence with their children without diminishing their own existence. Without you, your children would not exist. Both the sharing and the shared existence continue to exist, whether or not the other existence continues to exist. Multi-cellular beings reproduce by having offspring. In mammals, the ovum and sperm are complex single-cell organisms that have some of the characteristics of life, such as movement and some awareness, but cannot replicate. They are generated from full-life adults and generate a life force as a result of the union of the two partial life forces.

When the sperm invades the ovum, the combination becomes a new life force with awareness and the ability to react to conditions that produce development. The DNA acts as a blueprint, but the DNA does not produce the adult any more than an engineer's drawings produce an automobile.

The awareness of the fertilized ovum is demonstrated by a bird's egg. It is fertilized before the shell is formed and laid after the shell has formed. It is kept warm throughout this time and does not start to generate. Birds lay eggs over many days so that development occurs some period of time after fertilization. The growing process, in which continued heat is present, is not due to a chemical process, or the egg would have begun to grow when the egg was forming still in the mother's body. The egg was continuously warm during its formation and did not develop. The fertilized ovum determines when the conditions for development are right. For mammals, the ovum is laid in a life-friendly environment. A plant's seed is fertilized, but does not start to develop until conditions are right for the plant to survive.

An individual does not have the power to create a full living being; rather, it requires the sharing of a physical act by both male and female, but does not require any creative or mental activity on their part. Although a new creation results, it is not due to a creative act on the part of the parents. It is presumed to be a creation of love. Although love may be involved, love is not necessary. (It is to be noted that all other forms of existence are created by creators.) The new child has an existence, a life that the parents did not create but shared from their lives—an amazing process, possibly a direct action of God. The reproductive process clearly emphasizes sharing. The new life has the same level of existence as the parents. It is a continuation of the first life and is a unique life.

The female is the source of life, producing an ovum that when fertilized, divides. Conception is not a chemical process. It involves the immaterial sharing of immaterial life. Our observation of existence, living or non-living, is that all existence in the world, whose origins we can observe, was produced by a pre-existing existence.

We cannot directly see the origin of the material that makes up the world (rocks, water, air) any more than we can see the origin of the universe. We are surrounded by objects, both living and non-living, showing intelligence way beyond our own. The complexities of the universe are beyond our imagination. Although much effort has been put into understanding the physical world and universe, and we pride ourselves on our acquired knowledge, we still know very little about the immaterial and life. The most plausible theories of the universe accept a beginning. It must have always existed, or it had a beginning. Those are the only options.

There are those who claim the universe and everything in it happened by chance. The common experience is that things do not happen by chance—there is always a cause. If we consider that the odds for the formation of the universe happening by chance are in the billions to one, it requires a leap of faith beyond imagination. Others say it always was. If it were always existing, it would have to be timeless, and to be timeless, it could not be changing, since time is the measure of change. Alternatively, to have always existed, it would have to expand and contract. However, the observed facts do not support either theory.

In fact, the evidence indicates the universe has been changing and expanding for billions of years and is still expanding. It has shown no evidence of contracting, and the odds are unimaginable that it happened by chance. The only reasonable explanation is the universe had a beginning. The Big Bang theory of the beginning of the universe still remains the best description of how the universe came to be. Although the Big Bang theory goes to a billionth of a second after time zero, it does not explain why or how it happened.

To summarize, we have observed that existence can be material and immaterial. All living existence, as we know it, is shared. All living existence loves its shared existence, and its shared existence has an independent existence. As complexity increases, the level of living existence (awareness, intelligence, appreciation of beauty, and the ability to love) increases. All material and immaterial creations or buildings by man or animals start as a thought or from the imagination and occur because of the builder's activity and existence.

The universe did not happen by chance nor did it always exist. The universe and everything in it had a beginning.

From our observations, everything in the world whose origins we can observe came and still comes into existence as a result of the imagination, activity, and the existence of a previous living existence. All creations of humans are the result of the creator's existence and intelligence.

Any observed creation has a lower level of existence than the creator. A human mind is capable of knowing the universe and therefore has a greater level of existence than the universe, yet it is incapable of imagining the universe. It took a greater mind to imagine and create the universe.

We can extrapolate back to the origin of existence, which, unless it happened by chance, must have been a process started by a primary living existence. As in physical science, from earthly observations, the factors are then tested by observation in the universe. We know gravity on Earth and test it by observing the effects in the universe. In this case, there is only observable life on Earth, so we cannot test it. However, the choices appear to be either by chance or a primary existence. If life occurred by chance, then there is no cause for life. If there is no cause for life, then life has no purpose and the principle of causality on which science and logic are founded does not exist. So, in applying our observations of living existence, as we know it on Earth, one would expect the same process would apply to all existence. Since there was a beginning to the universe, as we commented above, and all known existences whose origin we can observe were the result of an activity by a pre-existing existence, there must have been an existence to start; otherwise, the whole process could not have occurred.

A reasonable theory is that the universe and every-thing in it is due to the activity of a pre-existing living existence that has an independent existence. Let us call the pre-existence the prime existence. From the above, we conclude that existence is a creation of the prime existence; thus, all existence exists because the prime existence exists.

In our observations, animals have limited intelligence and ability to create. Humans have greater intelligence and capacity to create. In all cases, the creations are not as great as or greater than the creator. In fact, their creations (poems, buildings, etc.) are at an immeasurably lower level of existence than the creator.

It is to be expected that the prime existence, to be the source and creator of all existence, must have a level of living existence (awareness, beauty, capacity to love, and complexity) immeasurably greater than that of a human.

The complexity, beauty, and immensity of the uni-verse are awe-inspiring. The mystery of conception, the complexity of the infinitesimal, the beauty of flowers, birds, animals, and even the location of Earth in the universe, shows intelligence beyond us. The list of intelligence, complexity, and beauty is endless and gives a good confirmation of the above-stated theory.

I do not claim this as a proof, only a good theory that has a very high probability of describing the actual origin of existence as we know it.

"I AM WHO I AM" (Exod 3:14 ESV)—I AM EXISTENCE. This is God's description of Himself.

CAUSE AND EFFECT AND THE EXISTENCE OF GOD

Science is based on the acceptance of cause and effect. There must be a first cause.

The Chinese proverb "He who knows, knows how little he knows" is not questioned by any thinking person. Even the unthinking person realizes how little they actually know. To make the statement that God does or does not exist is a statement beyond the ability of anyone to make, using one's own knowledge and intellect. No hard scientific, mathematical, or logical argument gives an answer to this question. But it is a fundamental question. The view of the world, the universe, and how we live are dependent on the answer.

Everything has a cause, or it just happens. General observation indicates everything we can observe or be aware of has a cause. We do not accept chance as a real cause. We investigate accidents. We do not accept they happen without a cause. We investigate crimes, death, unexpected occurrences, storms, any event, looking for a cause. We do not accept that things just happen. We live in a world and universe where cause is accepted and depended on, not a universe of chance. Nothing is caused by nothing. To have a cause, there must be an existence pre-existing the cause—the causing existence.

The beginning of the universe must have had a cause or the universe just happened. But nothing just happens. So why would the universe just happen?

Similarly, the beginning of life had a cause. There must have been causing existences in each case. Without the causing existence, there could be no cause and, if no cause, no caused existence—just nothing. For every cause, including the universe and life, there must be a causing existence beyond our ability to conceive: The Causing Existence.

The universe definitely displays causality. There is cause and effect, not happenings. Science is so convinced of this that thousands of scientists and billions of dollars are being spent to discover more cause and effects, not happenings. Life and the universe were not happenings. I call the causes that caused life and the universe the First Cause: God. Is it not time for science to admit there are existences greater than themselves, a First Cause, a prime existence?

GENERATION OF THE SPECIES (EVOLUTION)

Science assumes humans derived from *Homo sapiens*. The distinguishing characteristic of humans is free will. There is no evidence that *Homo sapiens* ever showed signs of free will. Humans were a separate creation in the image of God.

As a scientist, but also as a human, I have considered the mysteries of the generation of life in the world. The scientific explanation of the development of life is the theory of evolution. According to science, life happened by chance, possibly in the turmoil of undersea volcanic activity. Life developed by natural selection. Natural selection is not a definable cause, but is rather something that happens by chance. Chance is not an explanation. Nothing happens by chance. There is always a cause.

I find it hard to accept chance as the cause of anything. As I stated previously, even an accident is carefully investigated to find the cause. Looking at the generation of the species, it appears to be a managed process to generate life in the world. One of the characteristics of life is growth. Many species grow and then disappear. A species would develop, fill the Earth, and then an extinction would occur. The major extinctions would eliminate as much as 90% of all life and make space for a new wave of life.

There were six major extinctions and five lesser extinctions. It is apparent that the generation of the species was managed with the driving force of the growth of life. God does things in amazing ways, as the universe shows.

The growth of a plant in a microscopic way follows the mechanism of generation of the species. Once the seed germinates, it continues to grow to maturity, although affected by environment and other outside factors. The generation of the species definitely demonstrates that once life occurred, it grew—growth on a grand scale— but managed with extinctions and other occurrences to obtain the desired result. Evolution theory describes the genetic changes that occurred as life grew. Certainly environment and other influences caused variations, but the overall thrust was growth. The observed activities of evolution were caused by the growth of life, not the growth of life caused by evolution. The driving forces of natural selection should be replaced by the growth of life. Natural selection cannot be measured or even clearly defined.

The often-used example of natural selection is that a bias caused by the bird's inability to see the dark moths caused the increase in the number of dark moths. In actuality, the soot from the factories was the ultimate cause. So ascribing the result to natural selection does not define a cause. In other words, there was a definite, definable cause for the increase in dark moths. It may be called natural selection, but that is ascribing the effect to chance, or a fudging factor. If there were no bias or no soot, there would be no selection and no change in population. What it does show is that environmental factors can affect a population and a change in a population can result in changes in future populations. All growth is affected by environment and other outside factors. Growth of life is no more definable than natural selection, but is more descriptive of what is happening and indicates a process, not a chance happening.

As generations progressed, the characteristics of life grew, from a microbe to a human. Complexity increased from the single cell to the complexity of the human brain. Awareness increased—from the awareness of a microbe, to the awareness of mammals, to the awareness of a human. Concern for others grew. A tree covers its seeds with a hard shell and drops them and has no further concern for them. A fish lays its eggs in a safe place, but has no other interest in its offspring. A reptile buries its eggs in a safe place. A mammal is concerned with its offspring until adulthood. Humans are concerned for their offspring for life. To be concerned for another is love. The capacity to love grew. Mammals are derived from the reptiles and are more beautiful than the reptiles. Birds are derived from dinosaurs and are more beautiful than the dinosaurs. The generation of the species demonstrates the continuing growth of complexity, awareness, love, and beauty, along with many other characteristics of life. Growth of life was a driving force of the generation of the species, not natural selection.

Growth continued in the generation of the species up to the development of hominids (man-like in upright walking with the ability to make simple stone tools).

They were hunter-gatherers similar to the primates from whom they developed. Life on Earth continued to grow and reached the level of the *Homo sapiens*, who appeared suddenly about 200,000 years ago in Africa. They were anatomically equivalent to modern humans. For at least the next 140,000 years, *Homo sapiens* showed increasing skills in stone tool making and pottery. The progress that occurred was essentially physical abilities and skills, not an increase in intelligence or the mark of a human free will.

The Blombos Cave in South Africa was dated to be occupied about 60,000 years ago. Tool making shows greater skill and more care. Shells with a hole bored in them, probably to make a necklace, indicate a greater awareness of how others see you. However, cats are constantly preening themselves. Most animals preen themselves, but do not have hands to make ornaments. The increased skill does not show intelligence or the creativeness of free will, but physical ability.

About 60,000 years ago, there appears to be evidence that *Homo sapiens* started an exodus from Africa that is claimed to have filled the world. It is presumed that these migrants were modern humans called *Homo sapiens sapiens* (from my point of view, there is no difference and no reason to give them a new name; it's a fudging factor). According to the archeological record, there was no radical change in lifestyle, only improvements in skills of tool and pottery making, and no evidence of the inventiveness of free will or increase in intelligence. To go from a mammal to a human is a huge jump and no such occurrence is observed in the archeological record 60,000 years ago. The *Homo sapiens* continued a mammal's life.

The distinguishing characteristic of a human is the inventiveness of free will, the ability to act without the restrictions of instincts. Such ability allows rapid change. No radical change occurred. The *Homo sapiens* were mammals, not humans.

About 30,000 years ago, cave art appeared. Art is a skill. Like writing, the intelligence in art is what the art tries to say. The intelligence in cave art could be messages. Animals do leave messages. Many animals outline their territory by spraying. Cave art does show some intelligence, but art does not indicate free will.

Since the *Homo sapiens* are anatomically equivalent to modern humans, it is difficult to tell the skeletons apart. Amazingly few skulls have been found dated between 60,000 years and 30,000 years ago. Those that are found still show the bow ridges of older skulls, although not as prominently. It's only in the most recent 30,000 years that skulls classed as *Homo sapiens sapiens* are probably human and look human.

The distinguishing characteristic of a human is a free will, which allows rapid change. At no point do *Homo sapiens* show signs of the inventiveness of a free will, but continue the slow development of physical skills. *Homo sapiens*, in 200,000 years, never learned to write, even though they had hands. Although physically human, they were mammals and were never mentally or spiritually humans.

Science claims humans derived from *Homo sapiens*. A skeleton cannot show intelligence or free will. Tools and pottery show skills, not intelligence or free will. I do not know how a skeleton could show intelligence without the ability to write and leave a written artifact, or design of a complicated structure, or a radical change of lifestyle. No such radical occurrences show up in the archeological record before the Neolithic Revolution. *Homo sapiens* never showed the intelligence and free will of a human. The major observable difference between a human and an animal is free will—the ability to make choices independent of instincts.

The Neolithic Revolution indicates that a distinct change in lifestyle occurred from hunter-gatherers to settled agriculture with changes occurring rapidly. From the Neolithic Revolution to today (only 15,000 years) the changes are exponential; millions of times greater than that which occurred in the previous million years. An explosive change in the generation of the species occurred, providing evidence of free will, not instinct—human free will.

Science cannot explain the occurrence of humans. There are many things science cannot explain (a thought, a dream, good or evil); therefore, we have to open our minds and look elsewhere. Genesis (early Judaic writing) does give an answer.

The writing of the Book of Genesis, the first book of the Old Testament, is attributed to Moses. Moses received the Ten Commandments from God and was inspired by God to write Genesis. Genesis gives a description of creation. It describes creation as a command given by God, "Let there be light" (Gen 1:3)—the Big Bang. It goes on to detail the creation of the world and defines the working week. Finally, Genesis describes the creation of man.

Genesis gives two accounts of the creation of Adam, the first human. The first account is what would be observed on Earth, that the animals were created before Adam. The second account is what happens when creating, from a mental or intellectual point of view, where Adam is created as a thought before the animals are created. In any creation, the creation begins as a thought in the mind; a mental activity. It becomes a physical creation later, when expressed in existing material substance. For example, a book starts out as a thought and acquires physical reality as a physical book later, when the thoughts of the author are expressed in existing physical substances, paper and ink. The paper and ink retain their characteristics and, in the process, become an entirely different and enhanced existence—a book. From an observer's point of view, the book came into existence when it was printed and expressed in existing material substance. Similarly, the first account of the creation of man is what an observer would see: Adam coming into existence, when expressed in existing physical substance—a *Homo sapiens sapiens*.

In the second account, God creates Adam in his mind and creates the physical substance to give Adam physical existence. The generation of the species was the physical generation of Adam, ending with *Homo sapiens sapiens* being the physical form of man. God took the image of

Adam and Eve (in God's mind) and expressed them in existing material substance; thus, *Homo sapiens sapiens*. "So God created human beings in his own image. In the image of God he created them; male and female he created them" (Gen 1:27 NLT).

A fundamental characteristic of God is free will and the distinguishing characteristic of a human is free will, thus creating the physical Adam and Eve in the image of God, using the *Homo sapiens* body as physical substance. The *Homo sapiens* body, like the paper and ink of a book, still retains the characteristics of *Homo sapiens*, but in an enhanced state and under the control of a human mind, created in the image of God, demonstrated by a free will. Offspring are still generated by the *Homo sapiens'* body and are a continuation of the first life. Although the body, when developing, goes through various physical stages, the mind, having been created in the image of God, is spiritual and is not displayed by the physical. The image of God must be present, or the embryo would not result in a human. This is demonstrated by the difference in the development of human child and a mammal child. The human child is born helpless. Other mammals are not born helpless, although they are produced by the same process as the human.

The *Homo sapiens* that became Adam was an adult, the mammal body descended from mitochondrial Eve (occurring about 200,000 years ago), confirming that Adam and Eve were *Homo sapiens* raised to the image of God. Genesis specifically states they were created in the image of God; male and female they were created. The ordinary *Homo sapiens* were not created in the image of God. Adam and Eve were given free will. Humans were an entirely new creation, using *Homo sapiens* as material substance, formed from the earth, to give Adam and Eve physical existence. In Genesis, Eve was taken out of Adam, possibly a child of the *Homo sapiens sapiens* Adam, or she could have been taken out of Adam, as described in Genesis. In either case, Adam is the sole ancestor of all humans.

I believe the physical Adam and Eve were created about 16,000–17,000 years ago in Eurasia. Among the Jewish intellectuals, it is thought that Adam was created as a spirit at the beginning of the generation of the species and his spirit is shared by all humans.

It is to be noted that less than 3,000 years after the Neolithic Revolution, Noah built an ark the size of a current cruise ship. *Homo sapiens*, in 200,000 years, only made stone tools. Humans are a separate creation and are a different species than the mammal *Homo sapiens*.

I can demonstrate that the *Homo sapiens* never demonstrated a free will and therefore were not human. I cannot scientifically prove the creation by God. As science is confined to the material, science cannot answer how a unique being like a human, with an intellect and a free will resulting in a responsible creature, came to be. A free will and an intellect are not material and not in the scope of material science. No other existence had or has the intellect or free will of humans, even *Homo sapiens*. The only scientific statement I can make is that about 15,000 years ago the archaeological record shows a sudden, even explosive, increase in the development of the human, clearly indicating free will activity. I do not know why and, at present, have no scientific way of knowing. From a theological point of view, Genesis has an answer available to anyone with an open mind.

This, of course, brings up the question: what happened to the migrants from Africa about 60,000 years ago and did they fill the world? According to theory, the world should be filled with *Homo sapiens*, not humans. Certainly, when man occurred in Anatolia, there must have been *Homo sapiens* around who could not be distinguished from humans. There must have been interbreeding. This is indicated in Genesis 6:2 KJ21: "the sons of God saw the daughters of men, that they were fair; and they took for themselves wives of all whom they chose."

The sons of God were either angels or humans. Both angels and humans are direct creations of God. The writing is dealing with humans, not angels, so I believe the sons of God are humans; the spirit of Adam and the body of a *Homo sapiens*. In Genesis 6:3 KJ21, God states, "My Spirit shall not always strive with man, for he also is flesh; yet his days shall be a hundred and twenty years." Again, *Homo sapiens* are flesh, not spiritual.

Similarly, the human body is flesh and dies. So God is referring to *Homo sapiens* and the human body, which is a *Homo sapiens* body, because the sins are the sins of the body. As mammals, the *Homo sapiens*, without a free will, have no moral sense, but do have a man's body from which the human's body is derived and would be an easy mark for unscrupulous humans. The human body and the *Homo sapiens* body are both of the same ancestry and can reproduce. The offspring would probably have a corrupted genome—the reason for Noah's flood. Noah is referred to in Genesis as pure, an uncorrupted genome.

Noah's Flood

Did Noah's flood happen?

The tradition of a First Nations tribe in Western Canada is similar to all flood traditions.

The water having poured over the terrestrial disc, human dwellings disappeared.

The wind carried them away.

They fastened several boats to one another.

The waves traversed the Rocky Mountains.

A great wind drove them.

Presently the moon and Earth disappeared.

Men died of a terrible heat.

They also perished in the waves.

Men bewailed what happened.

Uprooted trees floated about in the waves.

Men having fastened boats together trembled with cold.

Alas, men were enclosed under the tent without doubt.[3]

This tradition implies that their forefathers were present. However, the basic tradition could have been brought by their forefathers from another culture, after the flood. The similarity of flood traditions indicates the latter. The archaeological record does not show any traditions of the *Homo sapiens* that emigrated from Africa.

---

3 H. Daily, "The Biblical Flood, Noah's Flood, the deluge of the scriptural Genesis record," Genesis Research, http://www.accuracyingenesis.com/flood.html

This is to be expected, since the *Homo sapiens* did not write. These are the traditions of recent cultures and can be traced back to 7,000 or 8,000 years ago, at the most, not 60,000 or 30,000 years ago.

If Noah's flood did happen as described in Genesis, it would be the twelfth extinction in the development of the species. The world would be populated by Noah's decedents, not *Homo sapiens,* as many scientists claim (possibly only 10,000 or 11,000 years ago—a very different picture than usually assumed). Carbon dating is being questioned by many scientists. Another factor is calibration. Written history only goes back to approximately 6,000 years ago, so dates of tens of thousands of years are huge extrapolations. No credibility is given to the scriptures, the earliest of written history, because it is said to be inspired by God—a limited and biased vision.

If a large asteroid travelling at thousands of miles per hour struck the ice sheet in northern Canada, tremendous volumes of ice would instantly be turned into water. Huge columns of steam and debris from the impact would fill the skies. Ocean levels would rise drastically and suddenly, flooding coasts and much nearby land. The tsunami due to the impact would be thousands of times greater than the Indian Ocean tsunami in 2004 (due to an earthquake that killed over 200,000 and destroyed many villages). The impact would generate violent earthquakes, as described in Genesis. It would also generate a huge amount of heat that would last for weeks, continuing to evaporate huge quantities of water. The steam would condense as torrential rainfall, continuing to fall worldwide, melting more ice, and further increasing sea levels. The torrential rain of Hurricane Hazel in southern Ontario in 1954 killed many people, washed cars away, flooded villages, washed out highways and bridges—and it only rained for twenty-four hours. The continued worldwide torrential rain would cause flash flooding across the globe.

A comet is a huge agglomeration of debris, smaller asteroids and ice. It could have broken before it intersected the orbit of the Earth and have pieces hit Earth over many days. It would dump huge amounts of ice that would melt, cause rain, and sea levels to rise. Continuing debris and asteroid hits would cause tsunamis and earthquakes and generate heat, melting terrestrial ice—all described by an Indigenous tradition. Worldwide flooding would result from serious impacts of huge chunks of solid matter. A comet hit may fit the Genesis account well. In such a case violent floods, tsunamis, and earthquakes would occur, and landforms could be changed, even mountains formed.

There is strong evidence that a catastrophe did happen about 12,000 years ago, possibly at the end of the last ice age. The Gulf of Mexico contains foraminifera, a planktonic organism. They live on the surface and lock the temperature and salinity of the water into their shells. The shells are discarded when they reproduce and these fall to the seabed, holding a record of temperature and salinity. This has been happening for thousands of years. Analyses of drill cores from the bottom of the Gulf of Mexico show a drastic drop in salinity in the Gulf about 12,000 years ago. To drastically change the salinity and be recorded in the shells, the fresh water flooding into the Gulf of Mexico must also have been flooding into the Atlantic Ocean. So the amount of fresh water was not a flooding river.

The archeological record shows that the inhabitants of England suddenly left the island, presumably for the warmer climate of France, about 12,000 years ago. The climate was colder at the peak of the ice age and the land bridge was available earlier. A more likely explanation is they were washed away.

The Great Salt Lake in Utah is in a desert area with no major rivers. The lake must have been created due to a tsunami of ocean water flooding over the Rocky Mountains, hundreds of miles inland, as the Canadian First Nations tradition states.

The great stone sea anchors found in Ankara in Turkey were certainly stabilizers for a large watercraft. All point to the story of Noah in Genesis.

Wadi Hammeh 27 is an early settlement in the Jordan River Valley. It was last occupied about 12,000 years ago. It is generally thought that the inhabitants were messy people, since refuse and waste are spread across the floors. More probably, it was spread by a flood.

Excavations in Europe and Eurasia have shown a sudden, short warming period about 12,000 years ago that swept through the area. This was quickly followed by a sudden return of ice-age level cold that lasted for several hundred years, possibly the effect of a comet that did not melt the ice cap, but caused many other disturbances, including rising sea levels, as a result of the melting ice of the comet. A research group in England has found an area of 2,300 square kilometers underwater in the English Channel that was inhabited about 12,000 years ago.

The Grand Coulee Canyon in Washington State, with the unusual formation known as the Dry Falls of Washington, is the result of a violent flood about 12,000 years ago. It is believed to be a flood from a huge lake dammed by the ice age that suddenly broke free—probably due to a comet hit.

A recent paper provides satellite pictures of the ocean bottom in coastal regions of Washington State where prehistoric agricultural areas are visible. It indicates that advanced civilizations existed in North America during the ice age. There must have been similarly developed areas all over the world, although very few have been found. They have been covered with water or been washed away.

The lack of remains of settlements or structures pre-ice age or before the 12,000-year date strongly indicates a worldwide flood. The so-called archaeological hiatus, a period where little archaeological remains are found, indicates a period of little or no life on Earth—as would be expected after a worldwide flood. Noah, to have built an ark as large as a modern cruise ship, must have lived in an advanced society. It is unlikely that Noah's settlement and civilization was the only one that existed. There must have been many others, but no remains have been found. Most archaeological sites of early man are caves or deep valleys whereby evidence has not been washed away by floods.

Cave art and the Neolithic Revolution show the intelligence of humans, thousands of years before 12,000 years ago, and such humans must have developed settlements with structures other than caves. The signs of civilization are either underwater, covered by silt, or washed away. There does not appear to be any evidence of a major flood occurring since the end of the ice age, which is approximately when recorded history starts.

Excavations at Ur and throughout Mesopotamia found layers many feet thick of silt at the bottom of the site. Signs of human habitation were found below the silt, and then undisturbed earth; evidence of a great flood that destroyed human habitation.

Settlements like Gobekli Tepe and Catalhoyuk in Turkey, are considered to be some of the oldest settlements in the world and are dated at 9,000 to 10,000 years ago. These settlements were buried and have only been discovered in recent times. It is possible that the dating could be in error, depending on what was dated; the structures are stone and carbon dating would be ineffective. The sites were buried, not by later settlements built on top of them, but by large rocks. One site is filled with gravel. How did the stones and gravel get there, if not by a huge flood or violent earthquake? These sites are probably pre-ice age and were not located on the coast, so they were not drowned.

These structures clearly indicate that advanced civilizations did exist. The almost universal lack of such sites definitely indicates they must have been washed away or covered with water. The earliest settlements would have been on seacoasts, lakes, and rivers. If sudden melting occurred, ocean levels would suddenly rise, and the coastal settlements would be covered with as much as 90 meters of water in hours. There would be no time to move and re-establish settlements as the sea levels rose. Civilizations on the coasts would be wiped out. Continuing torrential rains would result in violent land floods. Settlements away from seacoasts would also be flooded and washed away, destroying all evidence of pre-flood civilization. Flash floods would not wash caves away, so cave art remains. The cave art definitely shows the probability of civilization after 20,000 years ago. Because of Noah's flood, all records of earlier times would be buried or underwater.

The dinosaurs became extinct by a worldwide flood due to an asteroid hit, but that is dated at 65 million years ago. Great Salt Lake could not have been around for 65 million years. Further, the dinosaur bones found in Alberta and Montana, and other places in the world, show evidence of being moved after the original drowning, and deposited by a later great flood. The bone pits that are scattered around the world are filled with broken bones of both warm area animals and cold area animals. A probable explanation is violent floods.

There is evidence of civilization after about 10,000 years ago, about 2,000 years after the ice age. There is little evidence of development pre-12,000 years ago, even though cave art shows definite signs of humanity about 15,000 years ago (5,000 years is a big gap with little evidence of life, the very period when cave art shows development appeared to be accelerating). If tremendous worldwide floods occurred at any time, the indications of civilization would be destroyed. Buildings, tools, and processes such as tool making and metal refining would all be destroyed. Animals and humans would be swept away and buried under silts carried with the rushing waters. If Noah's flood was as severe as the one that destroyed the dinosaurs, advanced human life would similarly be destroyed. The survivors, Noah and his sons and their descendants, would have to revert to the Stone Age, as all the advantages of civilization would have been destroyed. Even if some humans survived the floods, there would be no life supports and most would perish. Animals depend on nature for life support and those that survived the flood could regenerate.

The Flood, the twelfth extinction, was the final act in the generation of the species and probably the last extinction before the end of time and the completion of creation.

Just because I am a scientist does not mean that I should ignore other sources of knowledge. Genesis speaks of the sons of God marrying the daughters of man. This could be the cause of the Flood: to eliminate contaminated genomes, possibly to render the *Homo sapiens* extinct like all other hominids. Extinctions occurred eleven times before to eliminate outdated species. Therefore, in such a flood, it is possible that all human life perished except for those in the ark, and the human race started over. This required about 2,000 years after the 12,000-year event before settlements appeared. It would probably take that length of time to redevelop the human race after the Flood.

The ark would be 213 meters long and 35.5 meters wide (according to the Egyptian size of the cubit) and have a total floor space on three floors of 22,685 square meters—space enough for more than 45,000 sheep. The total number of species listed today is approximately 20,000. Allowing for pairs and clean animals, the fact that the vast majority of species were smaller than sheep, and birds would be on perches, I believe the ark had enough space. Remember, the Flood was not a normal physical event. If it occurred, it was an act of God; the building of the ark was at the request of God. It must have been a worldwide flood or why would God not just ask Noah to move to another area?

The geological effects of a second worldwide flood would be similar to the first that killed the dinosaurs. Unless carefully looked for, it would not be noticed. Utah's Salt Lake and the displacement of the dinosaurs' bones indicate a later worldwide flood. Although the Ice Age or the effects of a comet or asteroid appeared to end by 12,000 years ago, ice-age cold suddenly returned, lasting for at least several hundred years. This is confirmed by excavations in Eurasia, mentioned earlier. The conditions that caused the Ice Age still existed after the asteroid hit. It appears that something interfered with the normal course of events.

Jericho is the earliest evidence of a continuously settled civilization (starting about 9,000 years ago), and it obviously was not destroyed by a worldwide flood.

This indicates that Noah's flood did not occur since the Ice Age. I believe that Noah's flood did happen, probably 12,000 years ago, caused by an asteroid or comet hit. If a concerted effort were undertaken to find Noah's flood, it would be found. It probably occurred towards the end of the last ice age and was a worldwide flood, an extinction, as Genesis reports.

The Genesis account of the flood is not the only biblical reference. It is repeated in Wisdom 10:4, 14:6; 1 Peter 3:20; and 2 Peter 2:5–6. It is also confirmed in Matthew 24:38–39 and Luke 17:26–28 when Jesus compares the destruction of man in Noah's flood to the destruction at the end of the world.

According to Genesis, it rained for 40 days and nights. It is also mentioned that the waters of the deep (ground water) were released with boiling water. The sun was darkened, probably by clouds of steam and debris of the comet blocking the sun. It took seven months for the waters to subside. One may ask, "If it was worldwide, where did the water go?" Where it came from—back to the oceans and ice. Floods are caused by the displacement of water as a result of rain or tsunami, not by new water. Admittedly, Genesis was written thousands of years after Noah and details are undoubtedly exaggerated. Genesis and the other traditions all describe a widespread catastrophic flood. Noah was in the Mediterranean, which is almost landlocked, and may have been blocked by the earthquakes that followed the hit. In 12,000 years, landforms could have changed. The Andes in South America and the Himalayas are growing fairly rapidly. The oceans could be back to normal, but the Mediterranean could still be at flood levels.

Did this happen? Traditions of cultures worldwide all refer to a violent flood, in which people died and the land was destroyed; it could not have been a flooding river. The similarity of traditions indicates that a similar event occurred worldwide, or that all cultures originate from one culture that experienced it. Those living on sea coasts would experience rising ocean levels and tsunamis and would not survive to offer their experience. Those in mountainous areas would be more affected by torrential rains and the rushing waters, and may have survived. Earthquakes would not be everywhere, so only some would be affected by earthquakes. Not all people were on the side of the Earth where the hit occurred and must have experienced different effects. If the traditions arise from those who were there, one would expect a greater variety of effects. The South American cultures appear to have arisen long after the Ice Age and Noah's flood, but still have the same flood traditions. Noah and his family, although safe in the ark, must certainly have been aware of the cataclysmic events happening outside. If all life perished, the only ones to witness it were Noah's family.

When God put Adam and Eve in the Garden of Eden, He commanded them to eat of the fruit of the trees and the animals to eat of the leaves. He forbade the eating of flesh. God's plan was a peaceful, loving world. By Noah's time, starting with Cain's killing of his brother Abel, the world had become a place of violence. Genesis claims that God was so displeased with His creation of life on

Earth that He decided to destroy it and start over with a man who knew Him and walked with Him. There is also the problem of the Nephilim and the Sons of God marrying the daughters of man. The human genome was probably being destroyed. Noah was described as pure. I do not think this meant he was chaste, but it meant he was uncontaminated. It appears for these reasons God decided to destroy all living creatures, except those in the ark, who obviously could live together.

Genesis, like the sun and its existence, cannot be logically proven. Similarly, scientific theories cannot be logically proven. They are theories that may be useful but which are not necessarily fact. A scientist with an open mind recognizes that Genesis provides useful information not otherwise available and is of similar value as scientific theory.

A FREE WILL

The effect of a free will makes humans immortal.

God has no limit to his choices. He has free will. The vast majority of humans of all races and at all times accept the sun as the source of heat and light as fact, without it having to be proven or disproven. It is considered self-evident. Likewise, the vast majority of humans accept a superior existence beyond the material as fact, neither to be proven nor disproven. On the same basis as the sun, it is a self-evident fact that there is a superior existence.

Humans made in the image of God have a free will and have no limit to their choices. They have the ability to make choices, even harmful choices. No other living existence in this world has free will. All other living existences act according to their instincts. They cannot choose a different way. Humans are not limited by instinct.

Animals, even the most advanced primates (even *Homo sapiens*), have not shown any signs of free will. They react according to their natural instincts. They are not created in the image of God. Humans are created in the image of God, with free will.

God has a free will and with it, God, the Father, has a self-image. This self-image is infinite and thus God, the Son, is the Second Person of the Blessed Trinity. There is a love between God the Father and God the Son. This love is infinite and manifests itself as the Third Person of the

Blessed Trinity, the Holy Spirit. The Blessed Trinity—One God consisting of three divine persons.

Humans have a material and an immaterial existence like all animals, but are made in the image of God with a free will. As a result, they have a self-image—a thought, a real mental or immaterial image of themselves. No other living existence in this world has a self-image. A dog or other animal does not have a self-image. Animals do not recognize themselves in a mirror or photograph. It is claimed that some primates do recognize themselves, but this is recognizing a characteristic, not a self-image.

A self-image needs a free will to be able to make the decision to be what it wants to be. Animals, without a free will, cannot make such a decision. A cat cannot act like a dog. A cat acts like a cat.

A human child quickly becomes aware of itself and starts to build an image of itself. To make a free-will decision, one needs to know what one wants. You must have an image in your mind of your likes and dislikes, an image of who you are or who you want to be. This image defines how you live and how you deal with others. Others deal with your mind, the real you, your self-image, not your body. The self-image has real existence, but does not have a material existence. It has a real mental or immaterial existence.

Your self-image gives your life force, your immaterial soul, a personality and gives you a real identity. When your physical body malfunctions, it dies, like any animal. An animal life force without a self-image has no identity, so its soul has no identity, and there is no way we can know what happens to it. It effectively ceases to exist. Your life force has an identity, your self-image, and it is the real you. You have a real immaterial existence.

Since the real you is not material, your material body dies a physical death, but not an immaterial or spiritual death. The immaterial soul or mind has a real immaterial existence (your self-image) that identifies your soul as the real you that others see and deal with. There is no reason for it to die or cease to exist. So your immaterial soul (self-image) continues to exist in time, but not in space. The self-image, as a result of Adam being created in the image of God, makes the human spiritually immortal with the characteristics or personality of the personally developed self-image—the real you. Human awareness and free will give humans the opportunity to choose or reject God. For this choice, humans, and possibly all creation, were created.

COMMENTS ON SCIENCE

In Genesis 1:3, God said: "Let there be light" and there was light. The Big Bang. God did not create matter, but light. Light is energy, and the equation $E= MC^2$ shows that light is energy, and C the speed of light involves time. Matter resulted. So matter is a characteristic of light and time.

As a scientist in my later years, I have become aware that science has made great advances in understanding nature, but to a great extent, it is all theory. Very little is solid fact; the theories appear to fit the facts as we perceive them, but the perceived facts do not include the immaterial, which certainly also exists. Is some of the unexplained, such as dark matter, involved with the immaterial and time? I wonder what the theories of the universe would look like if the immaterial were included in our theories.

Science is based on observation by humans. We readily observe length, width, height, and time—four dimensions. However, we cannot envision four dimensions. We can recognize a static space condition where the space dimensions are not changing, but we cannot observe a static time. As we are observing, a static state time is still flowing. We can observe the rate of change of time. We can recognize current time, and we can recognize past time. Future time we cannot recognize, but the future is there the moment we move into it, so the future is connected and based on the present. And we obviously cannot envision yet another dimension—the immaterial. Time is not really a dimension, but a factor. Similarly, the immaterial is a factor. We can recognize three dimensions while ignoring time and the immaterial.

This basically is what science has done with its theories of the universe. The factors of time and the immaterial are essentially ignored as they are hard to deal with. However, time is flowing and space is expanding; therefore, the picture presented today will probably not be the same as tomorrow. The universe itself may not be involved with the immaterial, but the immaterial uses space-time as a vehicle, since the immaterial exists in time and not in space. The universe was probably created to support immaterial life that is expressed in matter.

Time is more fundamental than space. All existence that we are aware of exists in time. Without time, there would appear to be no perceivable existence. A living being has a material body that exists in space-time and a specific immaterial life force that exists in time, not in space. The immaterial life force, shared from the original life, gives the body its living activities. The body exists in space similar to a rock and is an assembly of compounds like the rock, but its life force exists in time but not in space and cannot be touched, seen, or measured with our physical senses.

The life force is a specific immaterial existence, identified and defined by its physical existence or body and its activities. If the physical existence that exists in space is compromised and ceases to function, the life force that exists in time no longer has a functional space body as its identification. Without a physical identification, the life force can no longer be identified in space or time and appears to cease to exist in space. We have no way of knowing the fate of that life force. It was immaterial and existed in time, not space.

As mentioned elsewhere, the human has an immaterial self-image that exists in time, along with its life force. Therefore, the human life force, shared from the first human life (Adam's life), has a recognizable identity. So the human life force, with its identity, continues to be recognizable in time after the body dies, and therefore continues to exist in time.

Time is the critical factor in existence, not space. The universe is expanding not because space is expanding, but because time is continuing to flow and expanding space. We can visualize time speeding up or slowing down, but not standing still. If time stopped, then nothing would be happening, and we would have a dead universe—nothing could change. We can know the past and the present, but we cannot know the future. The future exists because time is continuing. We are continuously moving into it, and the moment we move into the future, it is there.

We are living in a space-time universe, and we have to account for time, which is more fundamental than space. As with anything observed, material or immaterial, there must be time. It is at least a four-dimensional universe and hard to conceive. This is overcome by introducing frames of reference. In this way, we can work with a four-dimensional universe. However, it is still not a complete picture. The frames of reference are in space while the fundamental dimension is two-dimensional time, past and present, not space. A thought exists, but cannot be described in terms of physical space such as length, width, or height. It is not in space. A thought exists in past and present time, with the possibility of existence in the future. The use of frames of reference does not cover this.

Time is not static; it flows and it is impossible to physically go back in time. We can view the effects of past time. Since thought is in time, we can mentally go back and, to a limited extent, go forward in time by anticipating future time based on past time.

Space was created when time was created and time is flowing, still creating space. Events that happen around us appear to happen in space since our senses can recognize space, and this occurs at a specific time. Time creates space as needed. Reviewing the example of the theory of relativity: If a cannon shoots vertically at the North Pole of Earth, the cannonball will be seen by a person on Earth going straight up and back down into the cannon. From Mars, it is seen as going up and moving sideways as the Earth moves. Here, we have two frames of reference, but also two entirely different uses of space, although one time event. The observation of space is dependent on the location of the observers. The experience of the observers is entirely different.

Space is a vehicle that time uses. When an event happens in time, the space for it to happen in is there.

Whether that space was there before the happening, the happening does appear to happen in space that was there before the happening. However, to be observed, it must be existing in time and space. All observation depends on the observer's point of view and location and therefore is not absolute. Science is limited to what can be observed by the physical senses.

All intelligent living existences have thoughts that exist. The thoughts, along with other non-physical existences, are not observed by the physical sciences. The convention that science is confined to the physical limits our understanding of nature. Science, to give a true picture, needs to include the immaterial. In accepting that the universe is in four dimensions, science has made the universe understandable to our three-dimensional senses by using frames of reference. We need another construct to understand the universe in both the material and the immaterial.

Existence is common to both the physical (material) and the immaterial. If we accept existence as fundamental, then time-space, material, and immaterial are all characteristics of existence. To completely understand the universe, we need to know what existence is. The real purpose of science is to understand existence. We need to understand the relationship of the material existence that exists in three-dimensional space and three-dimensional time (past/present/future) and dimensionless immaterial.

Dark matter and dark energy may be immaterial existences that keep the universe active. Like life, we see its presence in material existences but cannot see life itself. We arbitrarily separate the immaterial from the material.

This separation distorts our understanding of existence. God is existence. "I am who am" is God's description of Himself.

To understand the material and immaterial, we need to understand existence, and to understand existence is to know God. Science without God is looking at the shadows of existence, not the real existence. Humans are capable of knowing God, so science that accepts God is capable of discovering the complete picture, not the shadows. The marvels of the work of God can be discovered in detail, the prime purpose of science.

Thousands of people worldwide are involved in science. It is a means of earning a living, but it does not produce a material or tangible product; it produces knowledge. The knowledge helps humans to live better and longer. It also produces an understanding of nature, resulting in advances in technologies. Knowing that a star is one hundred million light years from us is of little practical use. The technologies developed to acquire this knowledge are useful. However, it is still useless knowledge when the vast majority of people have little interest in such knowledge. Governments and institutions of learning spend huge amounts of money and resources to acquire scientific knowledge. (One wonders if the billions spent on subatomic research are justified.) The purpose of acquiring knowledge in the first place is to learn how to live and how to deal with others. We also acquire knowledge to monetarily support ourselves and our dependents. It is also acquired as an enjoyment and in understanding life.

Pure science is acquired to better understand life, the world, and the universe. Since science is acquired by observation, the easiest and most obvious observations are made through our physical senses. Scientists have accepted the physical senses and devices that are controlled by the senses as the means and limitation of science. Although science has made phenomenal advances by this route, the immaterial is excluded, and there is much more that could be learned if science would include the immaterial.

Science explains life as a happening with no cause or purpose. Yet life is the most important aspect of existence in this world. It is immaterial, so physical attributes of life are investigated, but not life. Life is not a material existence, except for the knowledge of its attributes; nothing is scientifically known. Life, being immaterial, is ignored by science or attempted to be explained in physical terms.

The human mind is capable of considering the immaterial. A thought is immaterial, and the mind can handle it. I believe the main reason for ignoring the immaterial is Adam's sin—the desire to personally decide what is right and what is wrong—the sin of pride. Scientists are justifiably proud of their accomplishments, but pride can be carried too far and closes one's mind. To accept the existence of the immaterial opens up the question of a superior being (God), someone greater than the scientist. Many things can be explained if God is included. Some will argue that if God exists and created the universe, then there is no need for science. That is not a valid argument. Basically, all knowledge is discovering God.

History, for example, is studying man's reaction to God's plans. Science is specifically discovering God's thoughts and actions, not the activities of man. If modern science would accept God, there would be no need to dream up explanations like natural selection and chance happenings. The progress would be phenomenal and aided by God.

SPACE TRAVEL

There is a lot of talk these days about space travel. We are a long way from actual space travel. The distances are great and our speed of travel too slow. It took several days to travel to the moon, which is only 250,000 miles away. The nearest planet is millions of miles away, and the nearest star is four light years away (a light year is the distance travelled at 185,000 miles per second for a year), an unimaginable distance for human travel. Possibly a spirit could do this but, as a material human with the knowledge available today, such travel is impossible.

Space is expanding because time is expanding or, more properly, time is continuing. Time cannot decrease, time is always increasing. You cannot have negative time. You can talk and think about negative time, but you cannot experience negative time. Zero time cannot be observed because you must be in time when trying to observe zero time. Space is an expression of time. When we travel on Earth, we are essentially travelling in time and space, so our earthly space travel is time travel.

Unidentified flying objects (UFOs) cannot be from our solar system as the other planets have no indications of intelligent beings. UFOs, if they exist, would have to come from another solar system. The nearest system is four light years away from us. Even at the speed of light, it would take four years to reach us and then four years to return. If they are spirits, they would not need a vehicle in which to travel. There is also the scientific theory that nothing can exceed the speed of light.

For human space travel, there is another possibility. Humans are both material and spiritual. Up until now, the material has been superior. As a spirit, we are not in space but in time and are not limited by space. The faraway places are in space-time, so they exist in time as well as space. Humans exist in space-time and also our souls in time. Jesus said that if you had faith, you could move mountains. I do not think that Jesus made idle comments. I expect that if you had faith, it could be done.

This does not seem to be an action that could be done in space, but is one that is, rather, a time activity. Humans have the ability to act in time. All thinking is done in time, not space, and is independent of space. The immortal soul exists in time, not space, and your soul is the real you. Our bodies are vehicles for our souls. If greater emphasis were placed on our spiritual life and less on our physical life, we might discover amazing abilities.

To travel to a location is to experience the location. We can experience faraway places with our intellect. Our intellect can travel to the outer edge of the universe, so we are already, in a limited way, experiencing space travel in our minds. Our minds are attached to our material bodies. According to Jesus' comment, it seems possible to be able to use our mind or spiritual existence to do apparently impossible things—like major space travel. Many of the saints have done apparently impossible things, such as being in two places at the same time.

To truly experience our human capabilities, we have to become more spiritual and less materialistic, have more emphasis on the immaterial and less on the material. If we can concentrate on the spiritual, we may not need to build rocket ships.

GENETICALLY MODIFIED FOODS

There are many people who object to genetically altered foods. Most vegetables were at some time in the past genetically modified, either by man or nature. Grains are grasses. Most tree fruits have been specially grown so that the tree has to be grafted; it cannot be grown from seed. Almost all of our food has been modified at some time, usually under unscientific conditions. Scientifically modified foods are carefully studied and tested, and are probably safer than many foods in use. The fear of modified foods is more of the general fear of everything. It's the general inadequacy when there is no God.

Drones

Drones are flying objects that are controlled remotely or autonomously, often guided by satellite GPS. They can be programmed to automatically fly to any address and take pictures, drop a bomb, or do any other programmed activity. They can be used in many ways and can be of great help to humanity. However, they can be used in warfare or crime and have made the world a more dangerous place.

THE SOCIAL FORUM
MY EFFORTS TO
SAVE CANADA FROM
COMMUNISM

In the thirties, communism was the saviour of the world. The so-called learned (the media, many teachers, professors, radio commentators, and even movie stars), were preaching communism's doctrines. Tim Buck, General Secretary of the Communist Party of Canada, ran in several elections in Toronto and came very close to winning with 49% of the votes in the 1937 election. There were May Day parades with tens of thousands participating, singing the "Communist International" anthem. Frequent communist rallies were held in Queen's Park. Many meetings extolling the merits of communism were held in schools and halls. Ontario, and undoubtedly all of Canada, was set to become a communist country.

As a senior high school student at St. Michael's College during the Depression, I was encouraged to participate in charitable activities. Doug Bond, who became a very good friend, and I carried on the school's re-mailing of donated Catholic publications to isolated communities in northern Canada. Every month, we sent out several hundred publications. In my fifth year, I also helped out at Madonna House in the Spadina and Queen Street area. The house was set up by the Baroness de Hueck, who had escaped from the Russian communists, to provide assistance to the poor in the area. The person who looked after the daily operation was a young woman named Olga LaPlant. Olga introduced me to the Social Forum, an organization set up by the University of Ottawa, similar to the Catholic Worker in New York, to make known Christian social teaching in contrast to communist social teaching.

The Social Forum published a weekly newspaper, by the same name, condemning communism and pointing out the Christian approach to economics. It was on social matters, written by members, and included reprints of other social publications. We attended communist meetings, giving out our paper, and frequently got into threatening conditions, although no one ever got hurt.

The society had branches in Toronto, Montreal, and Ottawa. There were about 40 members each in Toronto and Ottawa, with more members in Montreal. Since the Montreal chapter was larger, we held annual general meetings there.

Our main activities were to inform the general public of the errors of communism. On Sundays, we sold our paper on the church steps, with the permission of the pastors. We also distributed our paper at communist meetings. Most of the members were active in the Sunday morning activity. The more dangerous activities were carried out by the male members.

For example, the Social Forum received an invitation to an anarchist meeting. Three male members, including me, attended. The chairman opened the meeting and started listing the location of firearms to be used in the attack on the legislative buildings at Queens Park in Toronto. Someone stood up and handed him a note. He then asked us for our credentials. We showed him our invitation. A discussion started between the members, and we beat a hasty retreat. We certainly broke up the meeting and may have ruined the trust of one another. The planned attack on Queens Park never happened.

On another occasion, while handing out papers at a communist meeting, some woman pointed me out and screamed saying I was a Trotskyite. A group surrounded me. I laughed at the accusation, and the crowd dispersed. Our members experienced many similar confrontations.

We held regular monthly meetings where we would set our objectives for the month. The Sunday morning paper selling was usually followed by groups from the different churches getting together at a coffee house as a social gathering. We also arranged with the bishop to allow us to have a dialogue Mass said once a month for our members. (A dialogue Mass was said in Latin, but the congregation participated in saying the Mass; similar to the current Mass said in the vernacular.)

A new apostolic delegate to Canada was appointed, and his first official activity in Canada was to recognize the Social Forum by inviting the members in each city to a meeting where he expressed the pope's approval and gave a blessing of our activities. Canada did not become communist, and the Social Forum was probably one of the reasons.

It was also a good place to meet your spouse. I met Elinor there. Elinor's brother Paul met his wife Marg there. Jim, Elinor's other brother, met my sister Jennie there. There were several other members who met their spouses. Several members became priests.

The war ended the Social Forum. And nothing has replaced it. Canada desperately needs a young person's group to advocate Christianity today. The volunteers to ISIS demonstrate the desire of youth to do more than play soccer or computer games. Someone needs to lead youth in working to make known the saving message of Christ. Parents should do it, but parents are too busy with other things.

Communism

In my teens, the Great Depression made living difficult for many people. Thousands were without jobs and a means of support, and depended on government handouts. Only lucky young people found jobs. There were groups of young men living in camps without any facilities. Many rode in empty freight cars (some even rode the undercarriage of freight cars, a.k.a. "riding the rods", when empty cars were not available), in order to move from place to place to look for jobs.

Communism was touted as a solution to economic problems. It was promoted by Russia as the dictatorship of the proletariat; a society where the workers ruled. It was supposed to be founded on Marxism, which advocates a classless society in which all means of producing wealth and all property are owned and controlled by the state, which of course, ends up in a dictatorship. Religion and allegiance to God cannot be permitted as the state is supreme, so religion must also be controlled by the state. But the abolition of private property is the abolition of freedom. For example, the farmer becomes a worker, not an owner, and most do as the boss, the state, tells him to do. It reduces humans to the level of a bee or ant.

Since the state is supreme, the individual is unimportant. So an individual who is not contributing to the state should at least be punished, if not eliminated, leading to the purges that occur in communist states. Stalin purged twenty million people.

Capitalism is often condemned, but is a good economic system if the capitalists follow Christ's teaching and love their neighbours. No economic system will work properly if Christ is ignored. Even Marxism would work if everyone followed Christ's teaching. Loving your neighbour is the answer to all worldly problems.

Russian Marxism became a terrible dictatorship. All communist or Marxist countries, because of the elimination of private property, resulted in a dictatorship where the workers, as a class, were important but the individual was unimportant. There are many who, due to shallow thinking, are still communists.

I had a personal experience of the "good life" with communism when I had a business trip to Budapest, Hungary, in the late 1960s. Ontario was sponsoring a sales mission to Hungary and invited me to go along. Hungary is a steel-producing country, and we were trying to sell our Thermocarb, an instrument that could analyze carbon in steel. Carbon content is vital to the final quality of steel and analysing the carbon content of steel was previously a slow and inaccurate process. My Thermocarb could do exceptionally accurate analysis in a minute, and was designed to be in the foundry so that the employees could quickly know the carbon levels as they processed each vat of molten steel.

I accepted the invitation with the trade mission, and went behind the Iron Curtain to an industrial show in Budapest. It was a 14-day mission. The first week was closed to the public, with the second week open to the public. I had nothing to sell to the public, so I only planned to stay for the first week. At the end of the first week, I went to the airline to arrange a flight back home. I was told that the mission was for 14 days, so I could not leave until the 14 days had passed. I objected, and the clerk grabbed my ticket, shoved it into a drawer, and stated that I would get it back when the 14 days were up. I asked to see someone in authority and was informed that the clerk was a commissar and there was no one of higher authority.

I talked to our mission leader, and he said he could get my ticket, but I could not leave until the 14 days were up. However, there was a Canadian embassy car that travelled every day from Vienna and back. I talked to the embassy driver, and he agreed that he drove to Vienna every evening and he would be glad to take me but pointed out that there could be some difficulty if the Hungarian officials found out. But the chances they would find out were slim. So I drove to Vienna with him that evening.

About two miles from the Austrian border, we were stopped by three soldiers with machine guns and ordered out of the car. The driver said not to worry as this was normal. They poked around under the car, under the mudguards, and then ask to see our passports and let us go. The driver said that he went through this every night. They were looking for people trying to escape. When we got to the border, there was a 20-foot-high fence with ploughed fields about 100 feet wide along the border, as far as you could see, plus machine gun towers. At the border, we drove into a concrete bunker, were ordered out of the car, escorted to a room, and the door was shut and locked. After about 20 minutes, the door was unlocked, and we were allowed to go out. Then we went into another room where our passports were examined, and finally we were allowed to go to our car. The back seat had been taken out and the spare tire removed. We had to put it back together and drove into the freedom of Austria. The driver said he went through this every day.

The mission leader was originally from Budapest and showed us around in the evenings. One evening, he took us to a night club. As we were sitting talking, everyone got up and lined up along the wall. Needless to say, we were surprised. The leader told us to line up. There were three soldiers with machine guns and a fourth going around looking at papers the customers were showing. When he got to us, our leader had a discussion with him and then he asked us to show our passports. That apparently satisfied the soldier, and he said that we could sit down. According to our leader, this happened frequently wherever there was a group of people.

There were lots of Russian soldiers, but I never saw them alone. They were always in groups. The story was that a Russian soldier who was foolish enough to be alone did not live very long. I did sell a Thermocarb at the trade fair. We never had any complaints and sold supplies to them for years.

Lost & Searching Youth

The forces of evil are rampant, promoted by the media, and accepted by the general public. No wonder we have terrorism and ISIS terrorist groups. They are so unhuman-like. They are even un-animal-like; very few animals kill just to kill.

We see thousands of young people joining ISIS and other terrorist groups. The terrorist groups are claiming to be doing God's will. I suspect the young people joining them are starved for religion and here is a group that is fiercely religious, with a reason to live or die. The society they live in is only secular and unsatisfying. It is the kind of world you get without God.

No one stands up for common sense. Movements such as marijuana, gay pride, homosexuality, promiscuity, and explicit movies on television do not encourage the activities of good citizens, enhance the state, or appear to be the will of God. So the young are joining those who seem to be fiercely doing the will of God.

FEAR

Many people are afraid of almost everything: global climate change (even though the climate has been changing for millions of years): genetically altered foods (even though most grains and fruits and many other foods were genetically altered many years ago); sunlight (the sun has been shining on Earth and people for billions of years); pesticides; nuclear energy; the ozone layer; the oil sands; drinking water; overpopulation; and many other fears. The human rights people have dozens more problems about which to be worried. These fears result in a feeling of inadequacy because one cannot do much, if anything, about these supposed problems. As a result, people live in a state of constant stress. The fears are mainly environmental, promoted by shallow-thinking media, scientists, environmentalists, and the United Nations by constantly reporting things that, in their opinion, are serious concerns. In a godless world, the UN attempts to replace God.

These are the rewards of godlessness. We never learn. The great godless (secular) nations of the twentieth century were Stalin's Russia and Hitler's Germany. The countries of the world are striving to be secular.

I believe many people have developed a conscience that is based on environmentalism and UN concerns instead of the two commandments of God as listed in Mathew

22:36-40 NET: "Teacher, which commandment in the law is the greatest?" [37] Jesus said to him, "'***Love the Lord your God with all your heart, with all your soul, and with all your mind***.' [38] This is the first and greatest commandment. [39] The second is like it: '***Love your neighbor as yourself***.' [40] All the law and the prophets depend on these two commandments."

This is a universal command. No matter what religion or sect, or who or what you consider as God, this commandment assures peace in any state or circumstances. Even an atheist can practice this way of life. He can still love his neighbour and, in so doing, be tolerant of his neighbour's views.

Many secularists are striving to ignore anything related to God or religion, setting the conditions for another Hitler or Stalin. To be morally correct is to be environmentally correct. The environmental god is not very satisfying and, as a result, many people live in constant stress because of these supposedly great problems.

For example, a woman I know keeps the blinds down because of the perceived problems of sunlight. The sale of bottled drinking water is a big business because of the fear of municipal water control. In fact, municipal standards are probably much better than the standards governing bottled water. Many use organic foods to avoid the supposed problems of pesticides and fertilizers. These same people are worrying about the increasing cost of food because the world's food supply is decreasing due to lower crop yields as the use of fertilizers and pesticides in food production become more restricted, especially in organic food. This leads then to fear of overpopulation, which leads to a fear-filled life that does not have time for enjoyment and love.

A feeling of inadequacy is also the cause of the irrational demands of safety. Fear arises because people cannot control all aspects of life, including their children's lives. This is to be expected because of the attitude that everything in their lives depends solely on them. They have been brainwashed by the supposed intellectuals, scientists, media, environmentalists, and politicians that they can control it all—they don't need God. These so-called intellectuals, blinded by their pride, ignore the Chinese proverb, "He who knows, knows how little he knows." The average person instinctively knows they cannot know all, and so the nagging fear or feeling of inadequacy results in constant stress. I believe this stress is the major cause of cancer. This stress disappears when one depends on God, who loves us and ensures that whatever happens will be for our benefit.

An important characteristic of God that we humans also possess is free will. The leaders of the world, who in many cases acquire leadership because of self-assurance and pride, freely choose to ignore God—and the sheep follow. God will let the world strive in the hopeless vacuum of no God. Without God's help, we see what a mess it is. All God asks is that we love God and our neighbour. In a world of love, what is there to worry about?

If people would put their trust in God, there would be nothing to fear. The current fear of everything is due to the loss of trust in God. With God's help, the inadequacy disappears, and we stop fearing everything. We can handle anything. Jesus said that if you have the faith of a mustard seed you can move mountains. Whether the problems we face are real or imaginary, we cannot solve them—but God can. God has been looking after the world since the beginning of time and has done a pretty good job of it, so ask Him for help and trust Him. Those who pray and live in the presence of God and use the two commandments of love, instead of the environmental commandments, live without stress and are not worried about all the environmental dangers. They know that God loves them, and whatever happens is within God's plan and will be for their ultimate benefit.

ATHEISM

One cannot prove there is no superior existence (a God) beyond the physical, any more than one can prove that there is a God. Therefore, atheism is a religion, a belief like any religion. It is not based on science. It is not in the realm of science to establish faiths or religions. Many small-minded scientists are atheists, assuming they are ignoring religion while professing a strong faith in the religion of atheism. The conclusion that there is no God cannot be arrived at by any rational process. Science cannot prove it. Science is based on observation of matter and even the most dedicated atheist has to admit that love, sorrow, hate, and thoughts are not matter. There is more than matter in this universe. The scientist who refuses to recognize the immaterial has a very closed mind, and the atheist who only accepts the existence of matter is a very illogical scientist.

The Big Bang is a theory and cannot be proven. If it is a fact, science cannot explain why it occurred. Similarly, the origin of life, a very complex existence, cannot be explained. The argument that life happened spontaneously in undersea volcanic eruptions does not explain how it just happened that the simplest of living cells are made up of hundreds of complex components. Many, who call themselves scientists, accept spontaneous occurrences as fact and are ignoring the very basis of science. Science is the explanation of observed phenomena. "It just happened" is not an observation; it is a copout. Any honest person, scientist or otherwise, will admit that they do not know the answer instead of assuming the happening just happened without a cause. This is not science; it is conjecture.

A better answer is, "God did it." This answer is at least an answer with a reasonable possibility of being correct. An agnostic is more reasonable than an atheist. He at least admits that he does not know. The atheist flatly states there is no God, a statement of a religious faith that cannot be proven. I find it hard to believe that a thinking person can be an atheist. It must take a very big ego to be an intelligent atheist. The vast majority of humans throughout history, and even today, accept a superior existence. The beauty of nature, the universe, the location of the Earth in the solar system. I could go on for hundreds of pages about the wonders that an atheist cannot explain while saying, with conviction, that there is nothing superior to me. Too bad more religious people don't have such a faith.

RELIGION

All people are aware of the brilliant object that gives us heat and light—the sun. It is generally accepted that the sun is an object independent of Earth. Many primitive cultures considered the sun as a god. It does have some of the characteristics of a god: it is not of this world; it appears to have existed forever; and, it is independent of humans, but necessary for life.

Even the most primitive people recognized that they could not satisfactorily live by themselves and needed others. They also found they could not understand or explain many of the occurrences that happened around them and were accepting of existences beyond their ability to know. As has been stated previously, the vast majority of people in all times accept the sun as the cause of heat and light, without proof or logical arguments for or against its existence. It is universally accepted as a self-evident fact that the sun is our source of heat and light. Similarly, the vast majority of people in all times accept a superior being as a self-evident fact. This cannot be logically proven, nor can it be disproven. All religions are interpretations of this self-evident fact.

Religions attempt to describe the characteristics, requirements, and our attitudes to the superior being or beings. Since the superior beings are not of this world, it is only by revelation that humans can know them. Some religious teachings are those of a wise person demonstrating how to live happily. All religions have prophets or wise men, inspired by their deity, to teach or instruct the populous. In general, religions developed written books of rules and practices.

Of the three monotheistic religions, only Christianity recognizes the Blessed Trinity, a natural consequence of a free will. God must have a free will, since he is not restrained by anything. God must know what He wants and, to know what one wants, one must know oneself. Otherwise, how could one know what one wants? A free will produces a self-image. God's self-image is infinite. Therefore, God the Son, the Second Person of the Blessed Trinity, exists. God and God the Son love one another and this love is infinite; therefore, God the Holy Spirit, the Third Person of the Blessed Trinity, exists. God, without a free will, does not make sense. The other monotheistic religions have not thought it through and reject the Trinity.

Christianity is the only monotheistic religion that advocates love of neighbour, even of one's enemies. It offers peace if the world would only follow it. The other monotheistic religions do not demand love of one's neighbour, so do not offer peace.

The earliest organized monotheistic religion still practised today is Judaism. According to their calendar, it was instituted by God about 4,000 years ago and is described in the Old Testament of the Bible. Christianity and Islam are derived from Judaism and are also monotheistic religions.

The Christian religion is based on the teachings of Jesus Christ. Adam was created by God as the first man and was given free will. He freely chose to reject a life in the presence of God in favour of the ability to choose what is good or evil. God promised a Saviour. (Judaism is still waiting for their saviour.) Christianity accepts Jesus, the Second Person of the Blessed Trinity, sent by God the Father, as a Saviour capable of satisfying God. Jesus, the Second Person of the Blessed Trinity by the incarnation, was born of the Virgin Mary and lived on Earth for 33 years. Many Jews accepted Him, but the authorities rejected His teachings and had Him crucified. Christianity is based on His teachings. He chose twelve apostles, and their writings are a record of His teachings and are contained in the New Testament of the Bible. His teachings can be summed up as: love God with all your strength and your neighbour as you love yourself. It is a religion of love. We demonstrate our love of God by following the teachings of Jesus. If these two simple rules were followed, there would be no wars, no crime, probably little poverty, and a world at peace, loving one another and loving God. Unfortunately, the world is not Christian, and many Christians only follow Jesus when it suits them. Like Adam, they decide what is good from their point of view. In general, practising Christians are nice people. They try to put love of neighbour into practice.

The other monotheistic religion is Islam. Muhammad was a warrior who set out a set of rules for his followers. Islam does not recommend that you love your neighbour and is not a religion of peace.

Why be a Catholic?

Catholics are one of the Christian religions based on the teachings of Jesus. The Catholic Church accepts the command given by Jesus to Peter (the immovable rock) to establish the church.

[18] And I tell you that you are Peter, and on this rock I will build my church, and the gates of Hades will not overpower it. [19] I will give you the keys of the kingdom of heaven. Whatever you bind on Earth will have been bound in heaven, and whatever you release on Earth will have been released in heaven. (Matt 16:18–19, NET)

Protestant Christian theologians maintain that the rock has a masculine and feminine case. The feminine case means an immoveable rock (a mountain), while the masculine case means a big rock that is moveable. The Greek translation uses the feminine case for the rock in the above command. The masculine case is used later to address Peter as Rock. Therefore, Rock means Christ, not Peter. However, these theologians are ignoring the remainder of Jesus' statement, "Giving the power to bind or loose." They assume Jesus is talking of Himself. As God, Jesus did not need to give Himself power to bind or loose. Furthermore, besides the possible translation errors, the Rock, the Catholic Church it is built on, is immoveable. The truth does not change. A tremendous power was given to Peter, the immoveable rock, a power that recognizes truth does not change, but humans are fallible, so an immoveable authority is needed. The Catholic Church has maintained its teachings for two thousand years while other religions change with the times. The Muslims are fighting among themselves because of different interpretations. They need a pope.

The other difference between the monotheistic religions is the consecration of the Blessed Eucharist, as described in Matthew 26:26–28, Mark 14:22–24, Luke 22:19–20, and 1 Corinthians 11:23–25.

[23] For I received from the Lord what I also passed on to you, that the Lord Jesus on the night in which he was betrayed took bread, [24] and after he had given thanks he broke it and said, "This is my body, which is for you. Do this in remembrance of me." [25] In the same way, he also took the cup after supper, saying, "This cup is the new covenant in my blood. Do this, every time you drink it, in remembrance of me." [26] For every time you eat this bread and drink the cup, you proclaim the Lord's death until he comes.

[27] For this reason, whoever eats the bread or drinks the cup of the Lord in an unworthy manner will be guilty of the body and blood of the Lord. (1 Cor 11: 23-27 NET)

He commanded the disciples to "do this in memory of me." Catholics believe the Eucharist is the body, blood, soul, and divinity of Jesus. Jesus gave his apostles the power to change bread and wine, spiritually, into the body and blood of Jesus. This power was given to the apostles, his clergy, not his followers. This power is passed on by the church headed by the Rock, the descendants of Peter.

Only the Catholic Church accepts the pope as the descendant of Peter, as having the power to bind or loose, to ordain priests, and to give them the power to spiritually change bread and wine into the body, blood, soul, and divinity of Jesus, thereby making Jesus present to all who receive communion.

These two events are ignored by all other Christian religions. Jesus did not come to Earth only for His day, but for all time. His comments were for all time. He did not forsake us when He ascended into heaven. He left us the Rock and the Eucharist, the protection of the truth and Himself spiritually. No other religion has the protection of the truth in the power of the pope and the presence of the soul and divinity of Jesus, the Christ, in communion.

VISITS TO NOTABLE SHRINES AND CHURCHES

I have had the opportunity to travel a lot around the world. One of my pleasures was to visit the great shrines and churches. I feel the presence of both God and the people who built and used them. There is generally a feeling of awe, peace, joy in the presence of their spirits. It is interesting to observe their architecture and their unique designs, but it's the presence of the spirits of people, angels, and God that draws me most. You may ask, why would God be more present in a church than anywhere else? God is infinite and eternal and present everywhere. But we are not so aware of God in the noise and haste of daily life. We can be silent and hear God in some places. Churches help us focus on God and the miracles of lives that he has blessed.

Saint Peter's Basilica at the Vatican, Rome, Italy

Martyrs' Shrine near Georgian Bay, Midland, ON

Basilica of Sainte-Anne-de-Beaupré, Sainte-Anne-de-Beaupré, QC

Shrine of the Rosary in Cap-de-la-Madeleine, Trois-Rivières, QC

Notre-Dame Basilica, Montreal, QC

Brother André's Shrine to St. Joseph (St. Joseph's Oratory of Mount Royal), Montreal, QC

Saint-Jacques Cathedral, Montreal, QC

National Shrine of the Immaculate Conception, MD, USA

Sanctuary of Our Lady of Fátima, Fátima, Portugal

The National Shrine Our Lady of Knock, Knock, County Mayo, Ireland

Rock of Cashel (St. Patrick's Rock), Cashel, County Tipperary, Ireland

Notre-Dame de Paris, Paris, France

Cologne Cathedral (Cathedral Church of Saint Peter) in Cologne

North Rhine-Westphalia, Germany *(amid the rubble of the war from World War II)*

Notre Dame de Vie (built in the year 42) in Vienne, France

I also visited and prayed in many other famous churches in Europe, the USA, and Canada.

UNUSUAL EXPERIENCES

The most unusual thing that I have seen occurred when I woke up in the middle of the night and my surroundings were as bright as at noon. The episode lasted for a few seconds, and then everything faded back to the dark night. The next morning, the radio reported a huge meteor had entered the atmosphere over Alaska, traversed North America, passing over New York City and ended up in the Atlantic Ocean.

Our Lady of Fatima, in her appearance in 1917, said that if the world did not turn to prayer, there would be another war more terrible than the present war (WWI). She said a sign of the next war would be a great light in the sky. I believe that meteor was the great light in the sky. Our Lady also said, if the world did not turn to God, there would be even more terrible times. The world has not turned to prayer. I think we are experiencing the predicted times now, with terrorism and world unrest.

My father, when living at the cheese factory, was to meet my mother's brother, who was coming to visit us. On walking down the stairs to go to meet Uncle Pat, Father saw himself walking up the stairs, and then the apparition disappeared. As he was driving to the station, the car skidded and rolled over. Because of the apparition, he was driving slowly and was not hurt.

My brother Ernie fell off a pier into water over his head. As I was about to jump in, he started crawling along the bottom and stood up where the water was shallow. His guardian angel must have directed him.

When visiting my mother in her last days, she was looking up and said to me, "There is the Blessed Mother. Do you not see her?" I believe she really did see the Blessed Virgin.

This reminds me of the story my mother told us about when she was a young girl and how she often went to an area called the Crags to pray. She prayed that she would see the Blessed Virgin. On one occasion, a great wind suddenly came up, she was frightened and ran away. She believed that the wind was from God.

Musing on Ghosts

Philosophically, I think ghosts DO exist. Ghosts are spirits, and there are good and bad spirits. They exist and they can make themselves visible to humans at times. I don't think they are in heaven or hell. They can be in either place. Heaven is not a place; it's a state. So they can be in either. I expect that a ghost would not be able to feel us or us feel them. I think that appearance has to do with people like my mother, who never appeared as a ghost, but she did make a phone call a few years after she died.

When my father saw himself coming up the steps, that was a ghost.

Ghosts are physical representations of spirits.

Ghosts are spirits of humans, not angels. Why do some humans hang about after death and others not? My mother used to tell me about a ghost girl who got on buses and rode a few blocks with many passengers. She would disappear as soon as she got off the bus. She was the ghost of a girl who died in a bus accident. Many people saw her, for years, get on the bus and off a few stops later and disappear. She was a real ghost, reliving an experience of her life that needed solving.

My dad tells a story of when he was woodcutter as a youth. At one time, his axe broke. He could not work without his axe. One other woodsman said that was not a problem and suddenly a new axe appeared, sticking in a tree. Dad took the axe used it to continue cutting trees. I do not think he kept it. But he often made the comment when he could not find things that the devil had hidden it and that God would help him find it.

My father never gave me any ideas of what he thought about God. He believed in God, as he sent us all to Catholic schools. He insisted on it. He claimed that he did not wish to go to church. His relatives always condemned those who did not go to their church. When he married my mother, they had to get married in the vestibule since he was not Catholic. So he felt that organized religion was not what God wanted or the right way to live. I must admit that I felt that going to heaven had little to do with going to church. God cares about how we live and love more than how we follow rules.

In Arvida, I had two good friends, Amby and Vic. Vic disappeared while swimming. He appeared a few days later at night and sat on the bed and chatted to Amby and said he had been hit on the head with a log. He told Amby to go to a particular spot in the river and they would find his body. The next day, Amby told the police, and they went and did find the body. Amby said it was just the same as Vic sitting beside him. After he had said where to find his body, he just disappeared.

That was indeed Vic, and he had a message to tell his friends. Definitely a ghost. I did not consider it unusual, just something that happens with close friends. I find that those who doubt spirits exist can ignore such events.

Elinor had such a vision after her uncle George died. One night, she woke up feeling that someone was choking her. It was her uncle George. She asked why he was doing that, and he said that she was the only one who ever loved him and the only one who could save his soul, but she was not praying for him. He asked that she do so. She did after that and never saw his ghost again.

That occurrence always made me wonder. It meant that he was dead and not saved, but that he could be saved by prayers. So you are not necessarily condemned to hell after death if someone else prays for you. He could not do it himself, but she could. It seemed to indicate that he was going to hell if no one prayed for him. As a spirit, you cannot earn merit according to the church. You need to earn merit while alive. So his prayers were not effective. I do not understand why this should be, but it seems to be the case. I think a spirit can still do good or harm, but perhaps with more difficulty.

Important messages come from our loved dead ones. This should not be considered as unusual, but as a normal part of life in which we do continue as spirits.

I am quite convinced that Elinor is watching over us and knows what is happening to me and our family.

Musing on Angels

My son, Peter, and his newlywed wife, Jocelyn, went to Switzerland on their honeymoon. They wanted to visit our homeland of Grindlewald. While there they took the mountain train ride to the top of Jungfrau and went hiking around the mountain top. While wandering, they got lost, and with the high altitude, they were soon exhausted and realized that the cold and exhaustion would kill them. They prayed for guidance, and a deer walked out of the trees and walked past them. They followed the deer, and it led them back to the train station. Without the deer, they would have died. I believe that the deer was an angel—a messenger from God, directing them to safety.

I have not met any such angels in my experience, but my son John tells me of many encounters that he attributes to angels helping him. They all look and act like regular people, but they convey messages to him that in retrospect show their message is an important one from God.

Angels are messengers and guides and protectors. John Jr. says that his guardian angel is excellent at keeping him alive since he should have died in many instances, but miracles happen, and he is still alive.

Not only did God create the universe, but He is actively involved on a personal level—each individual is important to God.

REFLECTION: GOD'S WORK IN MY LIFE

I reflect on our adoption of Deborah and how we all prayed hard for direction on this very serious choice. Events subsequently unfolded, revealing God's plan. When planning the business and holiday trip to the east, I had not originally included Quebec City. A late enquiry caused it to be included. I eventually sold a spectrographic lab to the Quebec Department of Health as a result of that call. Since we had to stop in Quebec City, it led us to stop at Sainte-Anne-de-Beaupré Shrine where we prayed for guidance from God about adopting a daughter. When we first saw Debbie, her name was Deborah Anne. I knew that she was to be our daughter.

God has directed me to live a successful and useful life. Whenever problems occurred, I asked God for help. The Thermocarb, although not the success I had hoped for, was still not a failure. Peter Maldenovich and I developed pin tubes for sampling molten steel. The pin tubes are still being used today in the steel industry. WearCheck is a company I built that separated from the rest of my company. It remains a worldwide success and now employs 3,500 people analysing oil in engines to dramatically extend engine life. Spin-off businesses like Activation Labs—which employs thousands in Canada, the USA, and Australia—are a worthwhile result of my efforts. Spectrographic analysis is now used as the main method of chemical elemental analysis in thousands of labs around the world.

In fact, many of the things I was prompted to do were primarily for the advantage of others. I was active in the Social Forum, fighting communism in the thirties in Canada when the media and intellectuals hailed communism as the saviour of the world. In Arvida, I arranged for a daily 5:15 p.m. Mass so people walking home from work could attend. I also started a boys club for teens to give them something to do. When we moved to Pine Avenue, I organized an altar boys club and a men's organization to attend to some of the parish's material needs. I participated in raising funds for St. Mary's new church. I was on the committee to raise funds for the building of St. Christopher's church. At St. Christopher's, I served as chairman of the Holy Name Society and was the first parish council chairman. I was an usher and minister of communion. As chairman of the parish ShareLife committee, we raised over two million dollars during the years of my chairmanship. In 2000, I was on the committee to raise funds for St. Christopher's renovations. As well as participating in church activities, I helped form the Canadian Spectroscopy Association and supported it for 15 years. I helped form the Canadian Testing Association, was chairman for several years, and continued supporting this association for many more years.

My vision of a good life has been that both family and God were more significant than money or fame. To live as

I felt one should, I have made many choices that were difficult, but necessary. I have often struggled to survive, yet always kept God and my family as the focus and always enjoyed the daily life and the good results that came from my efforts. For the most part, my life has been successful and joyful. This comes from following what I believed to be the right paths, not the easiest paths. I believe that what I was able to accomplish has helped improve life for all people. I believe that should be true for anyone who keeps their focus on serving God throughout their lives.

Elinor participated and was active in everything I did. She was also very involved in organizing the Catholic Women's League and was chairperson in both St. Mary's and St. Christopher's churches. She helped organize the Girl Guides at St. Christopher's and was involved in organizing the church community volunteers. She participated in raising funds for the Canadian Cancer Society and the Heart and Stroke Foundation. She also acted as a district returning officer in elections and canvassed for the Liberal Party.

Although Elinor's activity in the last few years was curtailed by brain damage and dementia, we never considered separating and putting her in a nursing home. We lived an active life together in the presence of God for more than 68 years.

Unfortunately, she fell and broke her pelvis while I was finishing the book *A Broader Vision*, and she did not recover. Although she has passed on, she is still present to me. I know that she is watching me and pointing out the corrections I have to make. I confidently look forward to being with her again.

DYING

We all have to die. At 98, I must be getting close to dying. It is frightening to think of the process of dying. It is a natural instinct to try to stay alive. One has to expect it and be prepared for it. At 98, I do not need much physical preparation. I have no responsibilities that need to be looked after and my funeral expenses are all prepaid.

After I die, I expect my soul will stay around for a time, as near-death experiences seem to indicate. Like a steam engine when the physical engine breaks down, the steam that made the engine work is still there.

I expect that I will have to spend some time in purgatory. What that is I have no idea. Since the crucifixion of Jesus forgave all sin, it must be some form of penance to make God's treatment of me justified. Purgatory may be the inability to really experience God before the end of time. I wonder what happened to Lazarus while he was dead. Jesus said he was asleep. However, the communion of saints assures us that we are aware and not asleep until the end of time. Elinor, my son Peter, my parents, and my brother and sister will be somewhere and will be praying for me. I will be existing in time and will see and communicate with them and others.

I expect that I will be able to know the answers to all the scientific puzzles, if I am interested. I expect my interest will be getting to know God and enjoying the presence of God.

Jesus told us that when He returns, we will be reunited with our bodies in a glorified way. The general judgement occurs at this time. I do not believe the general judgement will be an immense crowd, all listening to everyone's sins. The return of our bodies probably attaches our entire lives to our souls, so that anyone interested can know our life fully including the sinful and good aspects, and thus justify God's treatment of us. Jesus was united with His body after Easter Sunday. It was a spiritual body but could also act in space-time, as demonstrated by His appearances. Jesus also said we would be in a new world, probably a new creation, beyond our imagination.

FINAL REFLECTIONS

I have met many challenges in my business and overcome them with the help of God. When I retired, I built a cottage and wrote books—this being the fourth one. By actually looking for challenges, I have enjoyed an interesting and useful life.

I believe that a factor in my long life has been the satisfaction I attained from doing the impossible and doing what God wanted me to do. I believe I am still alive because I am still doing what God wants. I have lived my life in the presence of God by trying to keep God in mind with simple prayers (Jesus Mercy or Jesus Help) or discussing my problems with Jesus—often many times a day. All my challenges were done with the help of God, and I believe were given to me by God. I believe I have not died of cancer because I have led a life with lots of challenges with very little stress. I was doing God's will. What was there to be stressed about?